SOCCER
TACTICS TRAINING

General Principles
160 Exercises and Match Related Forms

Claude DOUCET

**Library of Congress
Cataloging - in - Publication Data**

by Claude Doucet
    SOCCER: TACTICS TRAINING

ISBN No. 1-59164-087-3
Lib. of Congress Control No. 2004096492
© 2004

Editing
Bryan R. Beaver

Cover Photo
Robyn McNeil

Printed by
DATA REPRODUCTIONS
Auburn, Michigan

Reedswain Publishing
562 Ridge Road
Spring City, PA 19475
800.331.5191
www.reedswain.com
info@reedswain.com

FOREWORD

Although technique is considered the key for success, it must be linked to tactical instruction to ensure that, in the end, a tactical culture has been developed from a young age.

As soon as a player involves a teammate in the game, as soon as a solution must be found for a game situation, as soon as a player needs to make a decision in order to move the ball, he calls upon his tactical insight.

Tactical insight is learned particularly thanks to unrestricted game related exercises whereby the player is allowed to freely use his creativity. Thus the coach does well when he provides for these training forms along with the customary exercises or other planned game forms.

Obviously the following facets of the game must be called upon:
• facets which represent a part of the strategy or the game organization,
• facets which determine the collective play of the team,
• facets which influence the tactical elements of each and every player.

Foremost the aim is to develop players who are technically well-grounded, possess a desired physical ability, are mentally strong and are tactically shrewd.

During the pedagogical process the exercises or game related forms are used as a pedagogical aid so that the players in the game can make use of them. In order for the instruction to be even more efficient, the coach ensures that there is a lot of variation in the exercises.

All of the exercises and game related forms written in this book were tested during training sessions. There are many variations presented so that every coach can adapt them to the level, age and goals of his team.

LEGEND

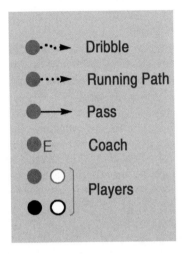

TABLE OF CONTENTS

INTRODUCTION

1 - TACTICS

The word tactics is used as soon as a player needs a teammate to bring the ball into play. It is the reply from a player or group of players to a certain situation during a game.

The best reply is dependent upon the technical competence of the player(s) and the adjustment of the player(s) to the situation. This adjustment is taught, instilled, and improved by means of training and repetitions of the combinations.

Tactics bring the game organization into action through the positioning and repositioning of the players that is appropriate to solving the game situation in an efficient manner. Tactics are dependent upon game principles, which make it possible for players to react in a homogenous manner and in the end find a solution for the given problem. The teamwork between two players forms the basis for this.

2 - THE GENERAL TACTICAL PRINCIPLES

The defensive tactical principles:
* disrupt the opponent's attack (disrupt, zone pressing)
* reorganize the team (reset the block)
* regain possession of the ball
* have a strategy in place for dead ball situations

The offensive tactical principles:
* successfully transition from defense to offense (bypass one or more defenders, help a teammate)
* ensure possession of the ball
* penetrate the opponent's defense
* finishing efficiently (numerical superiority in the offensive aspect, getting free from your opponent, asking for the ball, changing the rhythm).

3 - THE GAME PRINCIPLES

These are the basic rules of "collective technique" that enables the players to apply the tactical principles and finally provide for organization.

These principles are simple and become easy for the players to remember:
* whoever is the master of the ball, is the master of the game
* make sure of good positioning on the field, in the width as well as the depth
* take up a position and movements on the field
* make use of your zone
* assist teammates
  - offensive *(asking for the ball, supporting)*
  - defensive *(marking, taking up new positions, changing positions)*
* reposition yourself in order to:
  - receive the ball
  - take care of the marking
* continuously reorganize *(distance in relation to the play, distance between the players, contact between the lines)*
* look forward to the next action after a pass is given
* shift the play *(take the ball from one side and play it to the other)*
* make choices between the space *(advantageous to the attack)* and the pressure *(advantageous for the defenders)*
* change the rhythm
* do not push teammates forward
* make a choice between dribbling and holding the ball

GAINING POSSESSION OF THE BALL

Whenever someone talks about winning possession of the ball, someone must out of necessity talk about losing possession of the ball. Winning possession of the ball and the loss of possession are closely tied together and form the begin- and endpoint of the duality between attacking and defending, wherein every player contributes individually to the collective effort.
In these phases the roles are continuously changing whereby the struggle between attacking and defensive thinking determines the look of the team.

1. - LOSS OF POSSESSION

Soccer is characterized by a wide variety of situations where mistakes and inaccuracy are responsible for 85 to 99% of the actions being broken up, directly or partially through the handling of the opponent.
Barely 0.5 to 1.5% of the actions result in a goal being scored.
During the entire duration of a match a team loses possession of the ball on average between 210 and 260 times; shots that do not lead to scoring goals are also included herein.

The primary reasons for loss of ball possession are:

Type of Mistake	%/Match	Characteristics
Technical mistakes • bad passes • bad control	± 50%	20 to 30% of bad passes are blamed on a bad individual or collective control of the ball
Mistakes blamed on the opponent • offside position • pressure on the ball	± 10%	
Lost duels	± 15%	The previous loss of possession from dribbling (duels with the ball) could originate from technical, physical, and tactical reasons. It indicates the possibility to keep the advantage and ensure control of the match.
Interceptions by the opponent	± 15%	
Foul play (a violation of the laws of the game)	± 12%	This leads to 20 to 30% of the goals scored
Shooting that does not lead to the scoring of a goal	± 6%	

COMMENTARY

It can be seen statistically from past matches that the results are hardly determined by losses of possession such as: technical mistakes (50%), shots on or wide of the goal (6%), corners and fouls (12%), thus roughly 70% of the actions. Fouls, on the other hand, contain more risks because they bring the attack in a more advantageous position where they can deliver the deciding pass (25% of the goals scored versus 12% of the loss of possession).

• Observations show that loss of possession while dribbling has a connection to results. This message must be made perfectly clear to the players. During the World Cup in 1990, the teams that won the least amount of duels on the ball were eliminated in the first round.

• Loss of possession depends upon individual actions coupled with the individual technique of the player who is placed under pressure. Improving ball possession is consequently dependent upon teaching and improving the technical ability of the player. The coach should view loss of possession as a measuring stick and must look at the quality of his players and assess how much work must still be done.

• Teams that base their play on speed and playing direct passes lose possession of the ball much more easily. This type of play asks for speed in the performance of the actions, for the making of decisions and the taking of risks. This hampers control of the ball and the number of technical mistakes increases.

• Loss of possession becomes more predominate in the attacking zones, more specifically in the two zones in front of the opponents' goal. There is a real motivation for the players to defend in front of their own goal. So the team in possession loses the ball more as they approach the opponents' goal from the increased presence of defenders and the aggressiveness of the defense. The marking becomes stronger, the defenders close up the space in order to allow the striker less freedom. The pressure on the player in possession of the ball increases. The defenders are even more persistent in their tasks.

This is why the training asks for a limited number of players placed in a small space. The number of defenders will be dependent upon the desired intensity of the pressure that will be applied to the players in possession of the ball.

Tactical insight in this instance comes fully to the fore.

2 - WINNING THE BALL

Gaining possession of the ball:
take up positions so that in the given the time and space the result will be winning the ball back from the opponent.

Winning the ball has as its aim the prevention of goals being scored and winning back control of the ball.

Winning possession of the ball is a tactical plan that is applied to a collective organization. It is the fruit of a collective effort with the goal of:

♦ disrupting the attack and nipping in the bud every quick outburst from the opponent (zone pressing) with the result of giving the team the chance to reposition itself (reorganize the defensive line).
♦ Winning back the ball or forcing the opponent to lose possession resulting in a quick transition from defensive positioning to moving into attacking positions (pressing).

The defense against the offensive actions are achieved through individual or collective actions.

A - INDIVIDUAL DEFENDING

INDIVIDUAL MARKING

Every player picks up an opponent of his own and follows him in his own half. He hinders the opponent from receiving the ball by applying constant pressure.

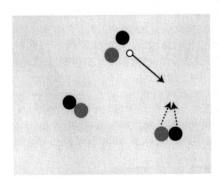

This form of defending carries many risks whenever the defender is by-passed.
The collective spirit can no longer be drawn upon and the offensive contribution of the defenders is restricted because they are required to keep an eye on their opponent.

DUELS
Duels without the ball (see the chapter DUELS)

INTERCEPTION

By this is meant a quick and bold action resulting in the winning of the ball. The player anticipates and moves into space in order to win the ball.

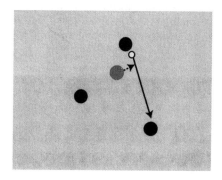

Interception is used:
* in order to get the play started quickly again
* whenever the opponent is strong technically
* in the case of a numerical disadvantage (2 against 1, 3 against 2)
* whenever the opponent waits for the ball
* whenever the field is heavy and it is easy to run down the ball

B - COLLECTIVE DEFENDING

INDIVIDUALLY TAKING UP A NEW POSITION: ZONE PRESSING

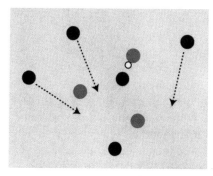

As soon as possession of the ball is lost, the player closest to the ball begins the "zone pressing" whereby he pressures the player in possession in order to give his teammates a chance to reposition themselves and to avoid allowing the opponent to begin a quick attack.
This defense is immediately applied in the zone where loss of possession took place (zone pressing), delaying the attacking wave of opponents and allowing for the reformation of the three defensive lines.

This individual action leads to a collective action.

15

HUNTING FOR THE BALL WITH A TEAMMATE

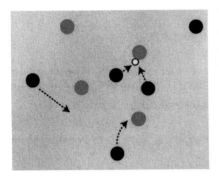

Two players at the same time aggressively press in the direction of the player in possession of the ball.

The idea is to win the ball back without making a foul and to begin a new attack.

PRESSING THE OPPONENT

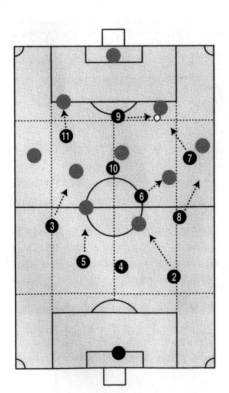

The goal of pressing consists of pressuring the opponent until he makes a mistake.

The starting of the pressing requires exact conditions in order to be successful. It is not useful to hunt a player who has time to bring the ball under control and, especially, if he has playable space in front of him.

The collective manner of the handling consists of closing off the playable space and not giving the opponent time to play the ball.

Pressing is the basis of an offensive action.

MAKING THE SPACE SMALLER

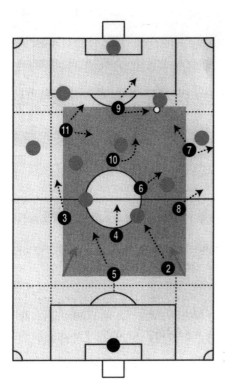

The aim is to limit the space between the players in order to obstruct the path to the goal for the player in possession of the ball.

Every player positions himself in a space in order to hinder the playing of the ball.

The use of the "block" requires painstaking organization and an advanced tactical insight, resulting in the closing off of the spaces and working to win the ball back.

In order to make use of this defensive system the players must show a great deal of trust in each other.

TEAM BLOCK

COMMENTARY

The best defense is not offense, but to play good defense. To this end, the player must have a game plan at his disposal in order to restrict the space and close off the playing areas; he must be able to fall back on the organization.

How does the efficient winning back of the ball transpire?
The required tactical defensive principles are to be specifically applied when:
- utilizing zone pressing,
- the defensive lines decide to fall back, the defensive block repositions,
- performing pressing defense

How does the defensive block reorganize?

The defensive block becomes reorganized by:

• the gathering of information by the players to understand the defensive actions,

• individually choosing new positions in function with teammates who stand in the defensive lines

The efficiency of the defensive system is dependent upon the coordination of the tactical goals for:

• the player in possession of the ball,

• the players that are not in possession of the ball,

• the possible paths of the ball

Statistics show that the winning team is better organized and gives more preference to winning the ball back by means of collective actions. They anticipate more of the opponents' actions and win more of the duels with the ball.

The victory is thus granted to the team that wins the ball back most often.

3 - TRAINING:
EXERCISES AND GAME RELATED FORMS

A - TRAINING OF BASIC ACTIONS

Gaining possession by an individual player is of course made possible by a collective regrouping and a large number of players in a small space.

The basic actions that make up a part of the whole range that the defender has at his disposal are:

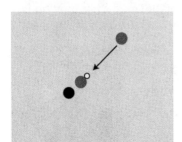

Jam up the opponent, then attack the ball (tackle, charge).

If the attacker is standing with his back to the defender, hinder his attempt to turn with the ball

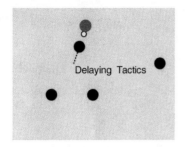

Delaying

If the attacker has turned with the ball, the defender employs 'delaying tactics'. He slowly runs backwards, thus delaying the forward movement of the attacker. The defender keeps an eye on the ball as well as the attacker.

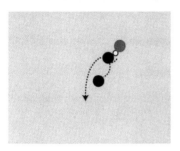

Supporting a teammate

The defender takes up a supporting position in relation to his teammate. If the teammate is beaten, he takes over defending the opponent. The teammate then moves into a supporting position.

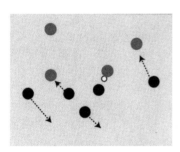

Zone pressing

A group of two or three defenders delays the attacking actions through collectively pressing, resulting in giving their teammates a chance to take up new positions.

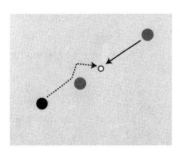

Anticipation

Anticipation in order to win the ball back has to do with getting a head start on your opponent, being quicker than he is, attacking every ball, and not letting him beat you.
Attack the ball in front of the opponent.

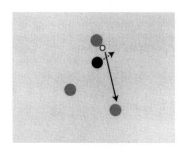

Interception

2 or 3 against 1
The defender attempts to intercept the ball close to the player in possession of the ball.

B - TRAINING DEFENSIVE AUTOMATIC ACTIONS

TAKING OVER THE OPPONENT IN YOUR ZONE

Across from an opponent without the ball who moves from side to side, let two defenders D1 and D2 alternate their positions either marking the opponent or taking up a new position.

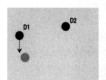 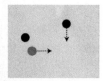 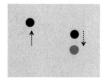 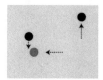

CHANGING OF THE ZONE BY TWO DEFENDERS

The central defender (CD) follows the attacker all the way out to the sideline. When the ball is played along the line, the outside defender (OD) chooses a central position. This should occur along both sides of the field.

 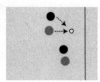 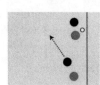 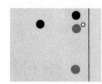

PRESSURE THE PLAYER IN POSSESSION OF THE BALL AND DROP OFF IN ORDER TO INTERCEPT THE LONG BALL

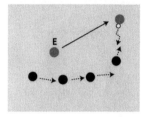 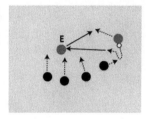 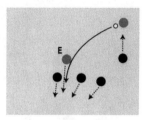

Pressure the player in possession of the ball in order to cut him off.

Move forward as the player in possession of the ball gives ground.

Drop off in order to intercept the long ball.

PRESSURE FROM THE DEFENDERS ON THE PLAYER IN POSSESSION OF THE BALL WHILE THE ATTACKER MOVES SIDEWAYS

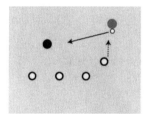 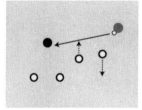 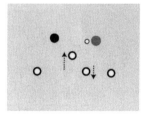

Pressure from the outside defender on the player in possession of the ball. He is supported by the right central defender.

The right central defender pressures the player in possession of the ball. He is supported by the left central defender and the returning outside defender.

The left central defender pressures the player in possession of the ball. He is supported by the returning right central defender. The right outside defender takes over his position.

21

PRESSURE ON THE PLAYER IN POSSESSION OF THE BALL AFTER A LONG BALL OR AN UNSUCCESSFUL BUILD-UP

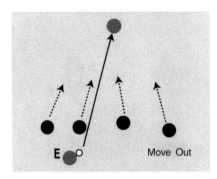

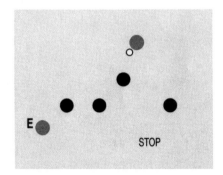

After a long ball from the coach, pressure the ball after the signal to MOVE UP.

With the signal to STOP, the forward movement ceases.

DROPPING OFF BY VIRTUE OF LOSS OF POSSESSION

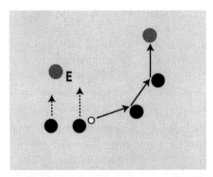

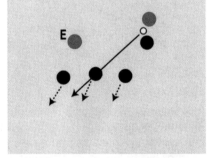

Build-up until the ball (voluntarily) is lost on the right flank.

Zone pressing on the right flank and the stopping of the defense at the moment the ball is lost, immediately dropping off diagonally in order to hinder a pass behind the defense.

MOVING UP AND DROPPING BACK WITH DEFENDERS CROSSING EACH OTHER

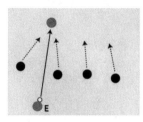 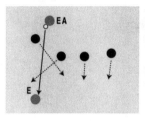 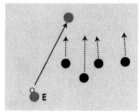

Pressure on the ball by the defenders after a pass from the coach.	Drop off with crossing of paths of the players.	Pressure on the ball after a backwards pass from the coach.

PUTTING THE ATTACKER IN AN OFFSIDE POSITION: TRAINING OF THE DEFENSIVE LINE

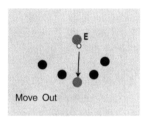 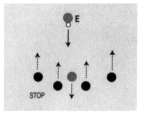 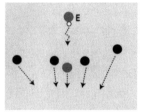

The player in possession controls the ball. The attacker asks for the ball. The defenders follow him.	About 33 yards from the goal a player yells **STOP**.	At the command **MOVE OUT**, all of the players move in the direction of the ball.

C - COLLECTIVE DEFENDING

Collective defending requires:
* the cooperation of all of the players,
* an organization,
* a synchronization of the running actions.

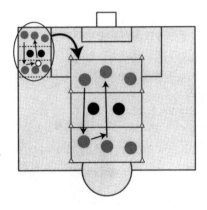

INTERCEPTION
- Field 11 x 11 yds., 8 cones
- 2 groups of 3 against 2 players
- 2 x 3 minutes - 2 minutes active recovery

The players in the outside zones play the ball to each other, and then to the team in the other outside zone. The players in the central zone try to intercept the ball.

Objectives: interception of he ball by the players in the central zone. Intercept passes, explosive movements.

Variations: limit the number of ball contacts to 3 per zone. Limit the number of ball contacts of the players in the outside zones.

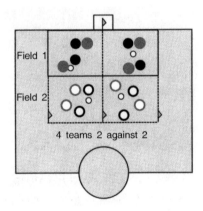

Field 1
Field 2
4 teams 2 against 2

WINNING POSSESSION, THEN KEEPING POSSESSION
- A large rectangle divided in two
- 4 cones or corner flags
- 4 teams of 4 players
- 2 against 2 on every small field
- 5 x 2 minutes - 1 minute recovery

The team that has the ball attempts to keep it as long as possible. As soon as a defender wins the ball, he changes teams. The players find themselves changing in the offensive or defensive numerical superiority.

Objectives: organize close to the ball and finally win the ball back and keep possession. Learn to play with and without support in different situations.

Variations: pay attention to the number of passes for the technically stronger players.

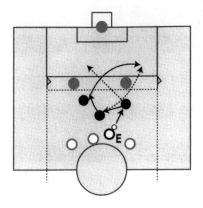

PLACING THE DEFENDERS AGAINST ATTACKERS IN NUMERICAL SUPERIORITY

• Half field, 2 corner flags or cones
• 3 or 4 teams of 3 players
• 3 against 2
• 5 x 3 minutes - 1 minute recovery

Defenders change at 3 minutes. As soon as the two defenders are in their positions (even with the cones), the attackers begin with a pass wide and make runs crossing each other. The attackers must watch out for offside. If the defenders win the ball back, they should attempt to play the ball to the next three attackers.

Objective: defending at a numerical disadvantage.

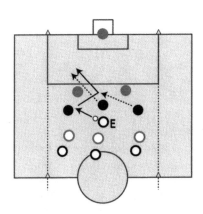

DEFENDING FOR THE DEFENDERS, PLAYING DEEP FOR THE ATTACKERS

• Half field, 4 cones
• 4 teams of 3 attackers -
  2 defenders
• 3 against 2
• 2 x 5 minutes - 2 minute recovery

The coach or a waiting player brings the ball into play. The defenders attempt to intercept and to position themselves between the attackers. As soon as the defenders win the ball back, two of the attackers become defenders. After a shot on goal the defenders remain in their positions while the attackers are changed with three new ones who begin from the middle line.

Objectives:
Attackers: score a goal out of a 1-2 or a 1-2-3 combination.
Defenders: playing in a zone. Intercepting the pass. Synchronize actions.

Variations: the defenders play for the offside. The time the attackers have is restricted. For example: 6 seconds.

25

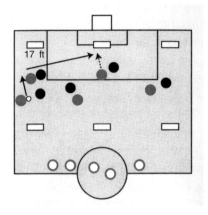

HIGH PRESSURE OVER THE ENTIRE WIDTH
* Half field, 6 goals 17 ft. wide or 12 cones
* 3 teams of 5 players
* 5 against 5
* 4 x 2 minutes - 2 minutes active recovery

Every team can score in one of the three opponent's goals. The team that scores remains on the field and plays against the third team.

Objective: high pressure
Variation: limit the number of ball contacts (for the technically strong players).
Commentary: the width of the goals compels the defenders to play high pressure.

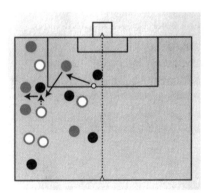

DEFENDING AFTER AN ATTACK WITH A NUMERICAL ADVANTAGE
* 1/4 of the field, 2 cones
* 3 teams of 5 players (red, yellow, white)
* 3 x 4 minutes - 2 minutes recovery

Two teams against one (10 against 5). The team that loses possession of the ball tries to win the ball back again from the other two.

Objectives: team not in possession of the ball: win the ball from the attackers with a numerical advantage.
Team in possession of the ball: keep up with the pressure.

Commentary: the emphasis lies with the availability of the players who are not in possession of the ball. The defenders are asked to find solutions in order to win the ball back (with two hunting the ball, pressing the player in possession of the ball, intercepting, closing off space, narrow the block, anticipate the pass).

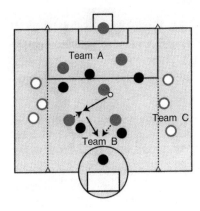

DUEL - WIN THE BALL - KEEP POSSESSION
* Half field, 4 cones
* 5 against 5 with keepers
* 3 teams: A (blue), B (black) - C (white)
* 5 x 3 minutes - 3 minutes active recovery

Do not allow any goals and success-fully win against 2 teams. The team that allows a goal against waits in the outside zones. Teams are required to change after 3 minutes.

Objectives: strive for offensive and defensive realism. Require total concentration.

Variations: the team that wins remains on the field. Score as many goals as possible within 30 minutes. Limit the number of ball contacts.

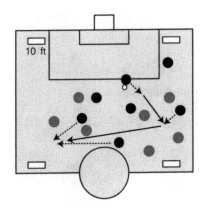

DEFENDING TWO GOALS
* Quarter field, 4 small goals or 8 cones
* 7 against 7 without keepers
* 4 x 3 minutes - 3 minutes active recovery

Each team attacks two goals and defends two goals.

Objectives: defend with a numeri-cal superiority on the flank where the ball is by leaving the other flank free. Begin on one flank and end up on the other.

Variation: may not score two times in a row in the same goal.

Commentary: place emphasis on the preparation of the space and placement of the block.

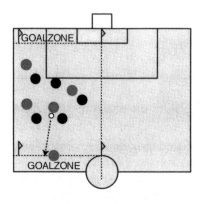

WINNING THE BALL - TRANSITION
 ◆ Quarter field, 2 small goals, 2 cones
 ◆ 5 against 5
 ◆ 4 x 5 minutes - 2 minutes recovery

A goal is scored whenever a player has the ball under control in one of the two goal zones.

Objectives: organize in order to win the ball back, transition to good ball circulation. From a defensive action, switch over to an offensive action. For the defense, pressure the player in possession of the ball.

Variation: the team that wins the ball back must first have it under control in one of the two goal zones. In order to score a legitimate goal, the team must then control the ball in the other goal zone.

Commentary: the applying of pressure lies with the positioning and availability of the players.

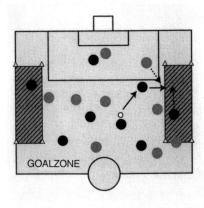

PRESSING
 ◆ Half field, 8 cones
 ◆ 8 against 8
 ◆ 4 x 4 minutes - 2 minutes active recovery

Bring the ball under control in the zones marked off by the cones (striped zones).

Objectives: individual and collective pressing. Learn to face up to these situations.

Variations: collective pressing with loss of possession. Restrict the number of ball contacts except for in the marked off zones.

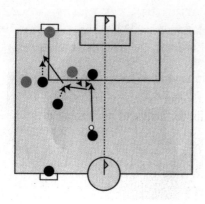

WINNING THE BALL - INTERCEPTION

- Quarter field, 2 small goals, 2 cones
- 4 against 2 or 5 against 3 with keepers
- 3 x 3 minutes - 2 minutes recovery

The team with the numerical advantage attempts to, by means of quick passes, attack by finding the "extra man". The defending team attempts to close off the space and anticipate in order to win possession of the ball.

Objectives: team not in possession of the ball: win the ball by closing off the space and attempting to intercept the passes between the attackers. Strive for interceptions.
Team in possession of the ball: attempt to reach an attacker in the free space.

Commentary: the emphasis lies with the availability of the players not in possession of the ball.

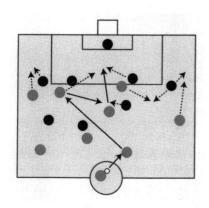

WINNING THE BALL BACK AS SOON AS IT IS LOST

- Half field
- 9 against 4 defenders and 3 midfielders + keeper
- 3 x 4 minutes - 2 minutes recovery

The ball is brought into play from the midfield line. If the defenders win the ball back (offside, duels), they try to keep possession. The attackers must pressure the ball and attempt to regain possession of the ball. Whenever the ball is played over the sidelines, it is brought back into play at the center spot.

Objectives:
Attackers: high-pressure as soon as possession of the ball is lost.
Defenders: zone defense or a mixed defense, keep possession of the ball under pressure.

29

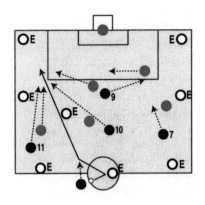

RESTRICTING THE SPACE
- Half field
- 4 defenders + 1 midfielder against 2 attackers + 3 midfielders
- 15 minutes

The coach brings the ball into play in all areas of the field. The balls are placed before the start of the exercise. The coach determines from where the play will begin again.

Defenders: training of the four defenders and the defensive midfielder.

Attackers: score from volleys and half volleys.

Objective: restrict the space between the defenders:
- on balls played over the flanks
- after the moving up of a defender
- after cutting off a forward

Variations: fast attack - direct attack. The emphasis lies with the work of the defenders and is not about not allowing them to get back into their start positions. Talk about the positioning of the players every time the play is dead.

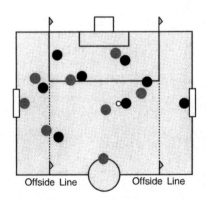

Offside Line   Offside Line

PUTTING THE ATTACKERS IN AN OFFSIDE POSITION
- Half field, 4 cones or corner flags
- 7 against 7 + keepers
- 3 x 4 minutes - 2 minutes recovery

Free play with the offside rule only in effect for the zones in front of the goal.

Objective: the defenders attempt to put the attackers in an offside position.

Variation: as soon as the ball is won back, look to counter attack as a team.

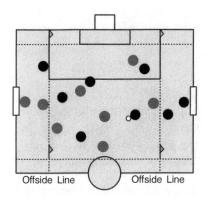

PUTTING THE ATTACKERS IN AN OFFSIDE POSITION + COUNTER ATTACK
* Half field, 4 cones or corner flags, 2 goals 5 yds. x 2 yds.
* 7 against 7 + keepers
* 4 x 4 minutes - 2 minutes recovery

The players are obligated to play over the zones on the flanks before scoring. The offside rule is in effect in the zones in front of the goals.

Objectives: defenders attempt to put the attackers offside. Play in the width, cutting off the strikers.

Variation: as soon as the ball is won back, look to counter attack as a team.

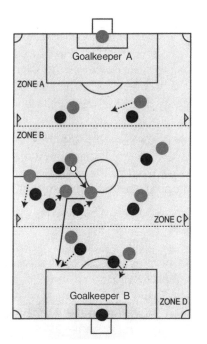

HIGH PRESSURE - FAST ATTACK
* Full field, 4 cones or corner flags
* 2 teams of 8 or 10 players and 1 keeper
* 2 x 15 minutes - 1 minute recovery

Change the roles of the players in each team.

Two players from each team are placed in zone A (two attackers and two defenders). The other players are free in zones B, C and D. Team A (blue) must make sure of good ball circulation in order to be able to reach the attackers. Team B executes high pressure to avoid allowing team A to get close to their goal. Whenever team B wins the ball, they look to counter attack quickly.

Objectives: high pressure to win the ball and counter attack quickly. Keep possession of the ball, advance the ball through a direct attack.

Variations: place a third defender in the defensive zone. Two attackers are allowed in the defensive zone.

31

PLACING THE BLOCK

* Normal field
* 11 against 11
* 2 x 10 to 15 minutes - 2 minutes recovery

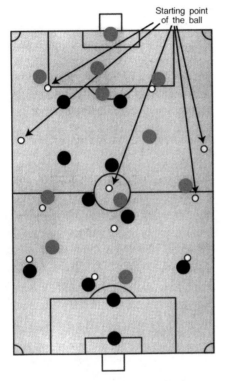

Starting point of the ball

Play is continued by means of:
* balls played from the goals
* balls that begin with the mid-fielders
* balls that begin with the opponent's defenders

Objectives:
* train the defensive positions of the midfielders and forwards.
* Pressing.
* take up new defensive positions.

Commentary:
This training heightens the watchfulness and sharpness of the players whenever the balls are placed beforehand and whenever the restarts - that are determined by the coach - are not predictable.

PRESSING IN THE OPPONENT'S HALF

* Full field, 4 cones or corner flags
* 11 against 11
* 3 x 10 minutes - 2 minutes recovery.

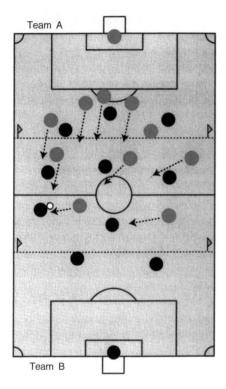

The ball is brought into play by the goalkeepers.
As soon as the ball lands in the attacking team's (team B) defensive zone - thus behind the middle line - team A must apply high pressure on the team in possession (team B) and make the defensive block more compact. The defenders play for the offside call.

Objectives:
* Win the ball deep in the opponent's half.
* Move the team block forward in an organized manner.

Variation:
Instruct the defenders in each zone.

Commentary:
The emphasis lies with the position of the players, the paths that they travel. These exercises use a signal in order to determine when the team will begin the pressing.

PRESSING ON A LONG BALL

- Full field, 4 cones or corner flags
- 6 + 1 keeper against 6, and 4 against 4 + 1 keeper
- 2 x 15 minutes - 2 minutes recovery

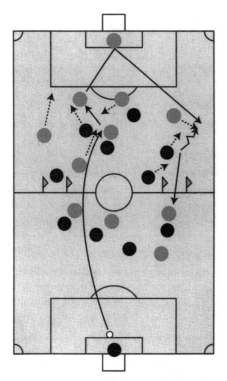

Long ball toward a high block: Long ball into the opponents in their half after getting rid of the defenders by performing an efficient pressing with 6 players (forwards and midfielders).

- If the defenders win the ball back, they try to score in the goals on the middle line or play the ball to the attackers in the other half so that they can try to score on the big goal.

- If the attackers win the ball back, they try to score in the big goal.

Objectives:
- Try to win the ball back as deep as possible in the opponent's half.
- Begin the attack in spite of the pressing.

PRESSING IN THE OPPONENT'S HALF

◆ Full field
◆ 5 + 1 keeper in one half against a team of 5 players
◆ 3 x 10 minutes - 2 minutes recovery

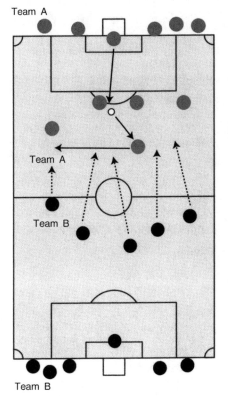

The goalkeeper throws the ball out into his own half and team B moves into the half of the defensive team.
If team A keeps possession of the ball, they attack team B's goal against team B, who defend their own goal.
If team B wins the ball, they attempt to score against team A and A must switch with the players behind their own goal.

Objective of the game:
For team A: move toward the opponent's half and avoid the pressure in their own half.
For team B: press against the attacking team.

Objectives:
◆ Keep possession of the ball, build-up, finishing.
◆ High pressure and active defending.

Commentary:
This exercise can be organized on half a field.

35

THE TEAM PUSHES FORWARD AS A BLOCK

- Full field, 4 cones or corner flags
- 11 against 11
- 3 x 15 minutes - 2 minutes recovery

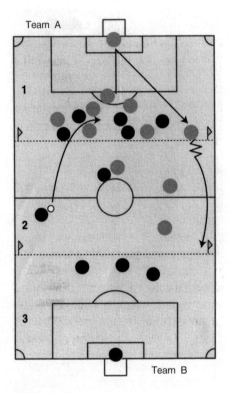

Spacing of the Players:
Zone 1: 10 from team A against 5 from team B
Zone 2: 11 from team A against 7 from team B
Zone 3: 11 from team A against 11 from team B

The play is started by the keeper with either a free kick or a throw.

Gain possession from out of a static defensive phase, followed by playing the ball forward and attempting to score.

As soon as team A has the ball in zone A, they join the players from zone 2 in the attack.

As soon as team B wins the ball back, they attempt to score with the maximum number of players allowable in the zone.

Objectives:
- Win the ball back.
- Push forward as a team.

Variation:
Instruct the defenders in each zone.

Commentary:
The emphasis lies with the positioning of the players, the paths that they take.

POSSESSION OF THE BALL

"Total soccer" doesn't have any secrets: it leans on ball possession and the positioning of the players on the field. Whenever a player receives the ball, he has many different playing options to choose from, and also whenever he makes the least desirable choice, the opponent should still be running behind the ball.

In order to play in this manner, people argue with each other over the quality the players must possess in performing the basic actions, including duels (30 to 35 %) and passes (60 to 65%).

Possession of the ball that is based on passes, making use of space and duels with the ball (dribble) forms a strategic element of the game that indicates technical, tactical and moral control.

1 - THE ELEMENTS OF BALL POSSESSION

A - THE PASS

The average number of passes in a top match ranges from 320 to 400. By its tactical and social aspects, the pass determines the collective play of the team. Central to every team is that they fall back on playing collectively in order to try to score a goal. The pass not only implies the players involved; a pass requires the involvement and the teamwork of the other players, combined with insight into the game, in order to make achieving a good pass possible (making runs to get free from opponents).

The pass is not only the performance of a technical action. A pass given is also the pass that was thought about, the pass desired, the pass realized, the pass evaluated.

Giving a good pass consists of a good ball given at the correct moment to the correct player; this requires the involvement of things learned on the training field as well as things in the "head" in order to anticipate the path of the ball.

A pass is characterized by its origin (place from where the pass was given), its length (long or short, know if it was < 20 yds. or > 20 yds.) and its direction (forward, right, left, backward).

The speed at which the player handles the ball depends on the number of touches it takes to control the before the pass is given. The number of passes that players do not control at the highest level averages about 25%.

The efficiency of a team is dependent upon the relationship between the goal scorer and the giver of the pass. In the chapter FINISHING THE ATTACK, it will be seen that 54% of the goals scored come after a good pass.

And finally, to improve the performance of his team, the coach will strengthen the collective play of his team and improve the tactical insight of every player resulting in passing that will lead to scoring chances and goals. He must stimulate the teamwork between the players.

The analysis of the passing of a team also provides information on:
• The social play,
• The player(s) who touches the ball the most (touches),
• The player who displays the most influence on the team (play maker),
• The conflicts in case there are many leaders,
• The offensive strategy of a team.

B - SPACE

Every player on the playing field has his own playable space. Outside of it he loses control of the ball and must run after it to win the ball back.

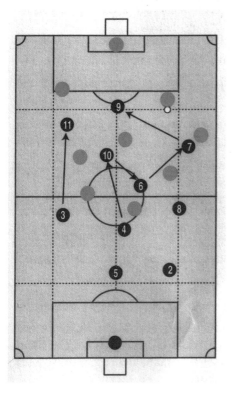

The overall surface area of the playing field is filled with the playable space of all of the players on the field and the free space between the players.

Knowledge about the relationship between the playable space and free space makes it possible to explain the duality of the attack - and the defense. The general principle of this duality lies in using the ball in the free space to the advantage of a teammate and through repositioning players and therefore neutralizing the space occupied by the opponent.

In the attacking phase as well as the defensive phase, every team is confronted with the proposition: make use of the space - neutralize the space.

This forms the variation between offensive and defensive actions, one of the starting points of collective and individual tactics.

The goal of the coach is thus:
• that his team in the **offensive** aspect realizes the perfect coordination between possession of the ball (passes) and occupying the space (positioning, giving support, asking for the ball).

• that his team in the **defensive** aspect is positioned so that they neutralize the opponents' space, or that the free space that is left open through poor positioning of teammates is covered.

From now on we will view making use of the space as the basis for collective play.

C - DUELS

Why are there duels?

Because the player with the ball has not played it off quickly enough or because the player who played him the ball did it in such a way that he did not get the ball in a free space at the moment he received it.

Whenever the ball is found in the playable space of two players, there is talk of a duel. The duel either means holding onto the ball (dribble) or winning possession of the ball. The ultimate objective for a dribbler is to create free space in order to pass or cross the ball, not another dribble.

2 - THE EFFICIENCY OF THE BALL POSSESSION

Ball possession has many objectives: take the ball away from the opponent in order to stop him from scoring a goal and make an opening in the opponent's defense in order to score a goal.

Observations have shown that complete teams have long periods with many passes (positional play) mixed in with shorter periods (direct play). They have total control and efficiently switch between these two options (positional play and direct play).

The positional play is an indication of good use of space and passing. The benefit of scoring goals. A good "passing game" is, as a result, necessary but insufficient to win.

3 - COMMENTARY

In order to improve possession of the ball, the technical level and the handling speed of the players must be improved. You could think that keeping the ball will increase the average time the ball is in possession during the ball possession phase.

This is actually very much not the case, except when the average time in the ball possession phase is constant, what the result may be. As a result just the number of actions and the speed of these actions is evolving.

Our observations confirm the words of F. CAPELLO, coach of A.S. ROMA. "Rebuilding of the mental preparation must be sought while the game is played even faster. Speed and improved technique, adapted to this speed, in my opinion determine the future of the game. The systems and formations will be derived from the increase in the speed of the ball on the foot."

4 - TRAINING:
EXERCISES AND GAME RELATED FORMS

A - POSSESSION OF THE BALL

Keeping possession of the ball occurs in a well-founded and active manner.

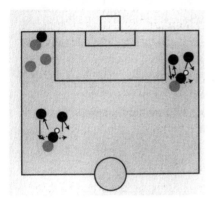

ONE TOUCH PASSING AND POSITIONING

- Half field
- 3 to 5 groups of 4 players
- 2 passers + 1 target player against 1 defender
- 8 x 1 minute - 1 minute recovery with changing players

The two target players play the ball to the striker who is positioned to cut off the defender.

Objectives:
- individual pressure.
- hold the ball under pressure.

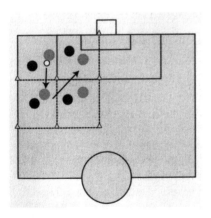

POSSESSION OF THE BALL - 1 V 1 DUELS

- 4 squares of 18 yds. X 18 yds., 7 cones
- 2 teams of 4 players with 1 player per square
- 3 x 3 minutes - 2 minutes recovery

The players play the ball to each other. A point is scored whenever five passes in a row are given.

Objective: keep possession.

Variations: a point is scored whenever the four players have touched the ball. The ball may not be played back to the player who just gave the pass.

41

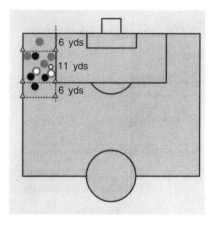

KEEPING POSSESSION WHILE AT A NUMERICAL DISADVANTAGE

 • Field of 6 yds. + 11 yds. + 6 yds. And 17 yds. wide, 6 cones
 • 3 + 1 sweeper + 2 neutral players against 3 + 1 sweeper
 • 3 x 3 minutes - 1 minute to change the neutral players

The two sweepers remain in their zone. The neutral players always play with the team in possession of the ball. Strive for sharpness with the first pass and duels with the ball.

Objective: keep possession of the ball while at a numerical disadvantage.

Commentary: the emphasis lies with the positioning of the players, giving support, keeping the play wide, and shifting the play.

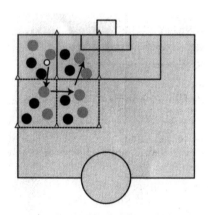

POSSESSION OF THE BALL

 • 4 squares of 18 yds. x 18 yds., 8 cones
 • 2 teams of 8 players with 2 players per square
 • 3 x 3 minutes - 2 minutes recovery

The players must play the ball to each other. A point is scored whenever 5 passes in a row are completed in different zones.

Objective: keep possession of the ball under pressure from the opponent.

Variations: a point is scored whenever the ball goes to all 4 zones. Make the playing area larger. A maximum of one pass per zone and then change zones.

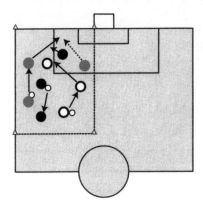

JUDGE THE POSITION OF THE OPPONENTS

- Field of 33 yds. x 22 yds., 4 cones
- 4 teams of 3 or 4 players
- 4 x 3 minutes - 2 minutes active recovery

The three teams play the ball to each other. Every team counts the number of successful passes. As soon as the ball is lost or is touched by an opposing player, the team must begin counting again at zero.

Objectives: judge the positions of teammates and opponents in order to give a pass. To look and to be seen.

Variations:
- limit the number of ball contacts.
- allow players from the other teams to disrupt passes.

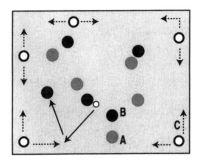

KEEP POSSESSION OF THE BALL WITH SUPPORT

- A smaller field of 33 yds. x 33 yds.
- 5 against 5 and 5 players in support
- 3 teams A, B, and C
- 3 x 4 minutes - 1 minute active recovery

Team A (blue) attempts to keep possession of the ball while under pressure from team B (black).

Team A receives help from team C (white) who gives support along the sides of the field

Team C plays the ball back to the team whom they received it from.

Team C positions itself only along the sides of the field.

Objective: keep possession of the ball with supporting players.

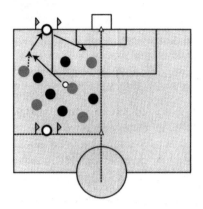

KEEPING POSSESSION OF THE BALL WITH CHANGING GOALS

• Field of 48 yds. x 33 yds., 4 corner flags, 2 cones
• 5 against 5 + 2 neutral goalkeepers
• 4 x 3 minutes - 2 minutes recovery

A point is scored by the ball being played to a neutral goalkeeper who then plays the ball back to the team that is in possession of the ball.

Objectives: for the team that has the ball: organize yourself in order to keep possession of the ball.
For the team not in possession of the ball: organize yourself in order to win the ball back.

Variations: change sides in order to score a point (may not pass twice in a row to the same goal). Limit the number of ball contacts (3, 2, 1).
Commentary: this game stimulates sharpness and insight into the game.

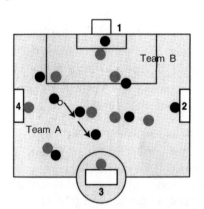

INSIGHT INTO THE GAME

• Half field, 4 goals
• 8 against 8
• 2 x 10 minutes - 2 minutes recovery

Team A attacks goals 1 and 2 and defends goals 3 and 4.
Team B attacks goals 3 and 4 and defends goals 1 and 2.

Objectives: training insight into the game, make use of available teammates.

Commentary: the gathering of information is important for a player. This game requires the player to look a step ahead.

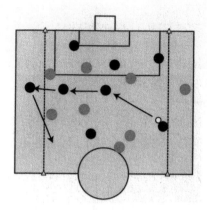

KEEPING POSSESSION OF THE BALL THROUGH THE CAPTAIN

* Half field, 4 cones
* 8 against 8
* 4 x 2 minutes - 1 minute recovery

In order to score a point the team must play the ball to their target player. This takes place in the zone behind the opponents' defense.

Objectives: keep possession of the ball. Pass and follow.

Variations: the target player may leave the zone. Change the target player after every point. Limit the number of ball contacts. Offside rule is in effect for everyone except the player in the zone.

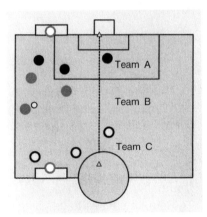

KEEPING POSSESSION OF THE BALL

* Smaller quarter field, 2 small goals, 2 cones
* 3 against 3 + 2 neutral goalkeepers
* 3 x 4 minutes - 2 minutes active recovery

Team B (blue) attacks team A (black) in a 3 against 2 situation (one player from team A does not take part).
If team B scores a goal, they get the ball back and attack team C (white).
If A wins the ball back, the 3rd player joins the play, team A attacks team C and team B becomes the defenders (in place of A).

Objective: transition from defending at a numerical disadvantage to attacking with a numerical advantage.

Variations: limit the number of ball contacts. Delay the actions of the third player whenever the team attacks.

BALL CIRCULATION IN THE ZONES

* Large field, 4 small goals
* 10 against 10 without keepers
* 5 x 3 minutes - 1 minute active recovery

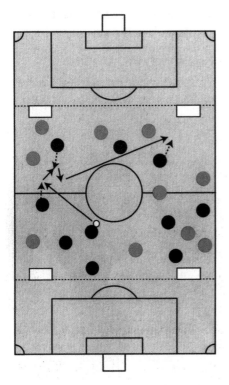

Each team scores in two goals and defends two goals.

Objectives:
* Attempt to by-pass the opponents' defense by quickly changing the zone or by moving the play.
* Look for connecting points and play there. Transition quickly from defending to attacking.

Variations:
* Score with the foot on one side and with the head on the other side.
* A legitimate goal is scored if the entire team is in the opponent's half.
* Forbid going into the center circle.
* Require the play to go through the center circle.
* Require passes to be given in all four zones before a goal is scored.

KEEPING POSSESSION OF THE BALL TO PROGRESS

- Large field, 4 small goals or 8 corner flags
- 9 against 9
- 5 x 3 minutes - 1 minute recovery

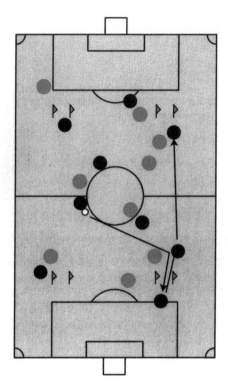

Score a goal in one of the other goals. The goal is scored whenever two players from the same team play the ball back and forth to each other through the goal.
As soon as the goal is scored, the team must score in one of the other goals.

Objectives:
- Collectively keeping possession of the ball.
- Try to draw the opponent to one side and then change the play to the other side.
- Defend with numerical superiority on the side with the ball.
- Strive first for a quick explosion, then a more direct attack.

Variations:
- Limit the number of ball contacts.
- 1 passes to 2, who looks for 3.
- Goals should be scored after a dribble.
- Alternate scoring in two goals.

TRAINING OF CROSSING RUNS

People strive for progression in the exercises, where the number of defenders is adjusted in relation to the intensity of the desired pressure and the technical ability of the attackers.
- training without a defender, with cones
- training with 2 defenders

Training with one defender is not recommended.

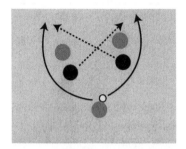

Crossing runs

Moving with crossing runs in order to allow a pass into the free space.

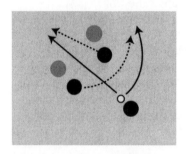

Crossing runs in order to create space

An attacker slips between two defenders while the other crosses behind his back.

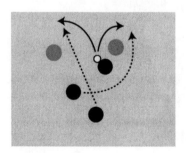

Runs behind the player in possession of the ball

Move behind the playmaker.

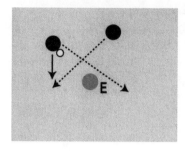

Crossing runs in the back

Give a deep pass in front of a teammate who goes to the ball, this is followed by crossing runs behind the coach or a player.

Through the position of the third player or of the coach using cones, many teams can perform the exercise over the width of the field.

These exercises can be performed toward a goal and ended with a shot.

C - LOOKING FOR THE SPACE

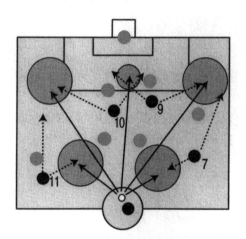

The free space

The movement of the players creates free space where the ball is received by means of long, short and crossed passes.

These spaces are found between or behind the defenders and midfielders. They are indicated by the five gray zones.

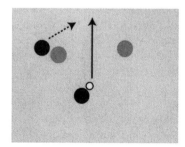

Principle

There is still an opponent in front of you; also there is still open space between two defenders.

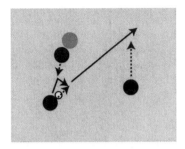

TWO SHORT PASSES FOLLOWED BY A LONG PASS IN FRONT OF A PLAYER IN SPACE

* Half field
* 2 against 1 + 1 player in the space
* 4 x 2 minutes - 1 minute recovery with the changing of the defenders

The defender marks a player who serves as support.
After a few short passes between the two players, the third isolated player is played a long pass into the space.

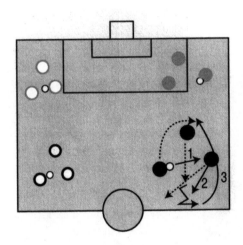

ASKING FOR THE BALL IN THE FREE SPACE

* Half field
* 4 or 5 groups of 3 players
* 1 x 10 minutes - 2 minutes recovery

Three players play a ball to a player who asks for it in the free space.

Objective: asking for the ball in the free space.

Variations: every player follows his pass. Two short passes followed by a long pass to the player who asks for it.

Commentary: Ask the players to make crossing runs. The players must never stand in the same line and must avoid running parallel. Play direct passes with anticipation around the player in possession of the ball.

Organization: Explain the exercise on the blackboard. Ask that the exercise is first performed at a low speed, then at a normal speed.

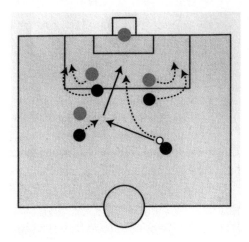

CREATE SPACE IN THE CENTER OF THE FIELD BY ASKING FOR THE BALL

* Half field
* 4 against 4 including 1 keeper
* 4 x 3 minutes - 1 minute recovery

The attackers ask for the ball over the wings in order to create free space in the center of the field.

Objectives: create free space, ask for the ball in the free zones. Make the right decision.

Variation: take the offside rule into account.

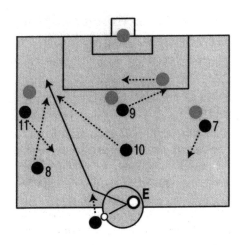

MAKE USE OF THE FREE SPACE: MOVEMENT OF THE FORWARDS AND MID-FIELDERS

* Half field
* 4 defenders + 1 keeper against 3 forwards and 2 midfielders

The wingers (11, 7) drop back in order to make free space.

Objective: Use the free space behind the poorly positioned defenders.

Variations: begin on one side and end on the other side.
Look for space during the play.
Free exercise, allow the attackers to find their own solutions.

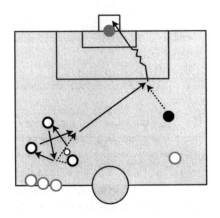

PREPARING TO CHANGE THE PLAY

+ Half field
+ 2 or 3 groups of 4 players
+ 3 x 5 minutes - 2 minutes recovery

Three players play one touch to each other (pass and move). After a couple of passes one of the players (the best positioned player) plays a long ball to a fourth player who finishes on goal.

Objective: Lure the defenders to one side in order to create free space for the striker.

Variations: two defenders against three attackers.
A defender joins in when the striker receives the ball.

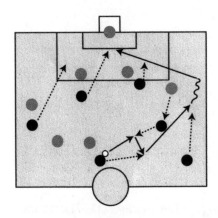

PREPARING THE ZONE IN FRONT OF THE DEFENDER

+ Half field
+ 6 against 6 + 1 keeper
+ 4 x 5 minutes - 1 min recovery

The player in possession of the ball waits for the support from the right midfielder, who comes back in order to make space by luring the defender to come with him. The right defender bolts into the space in order to receive the ball in stride. The coach begins the play from the middle of the field. Switch from performing the exercise on right side to the left side. After about 5 minutes the defenders and attackers change roles.

Objective: Passes and movement of the players become synchronized.

Commentary: The emphasis lies in the synchronization of the passes and movements.

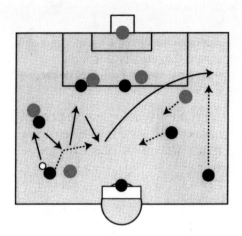

PREPARATION ALONG ONE SIDE - FINISHING ALONG THE OTHER SIDE

* Half field
* 5 against 5 with keepers
* 3 x 4 minutes - 2 min recovery

By means of short passes, the players keep the ball in an area of the field resulting in luring the opponents' block and creating free space.

Objectives: narrow the offensive block in order to lure the defenders into one zone and make free space. Disguise what is going to take place by making other runs.

Commentary: The midfielders and forwards attempt to conceal what is going to take place.

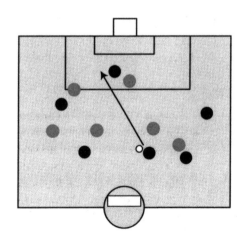

INITIATE SPACE: PLAYING BETWEEN PLAYERS

* Half field
* 5 against 5 to 8 against 8
* 5 x 3 minutes - 1 min recovery

Free play. At a signal from the coach the team without the ball stands still, as does the player who is in possession of the ball. The other players move further, resulting in the player with the ball being able to see them between two opponents.

Objectives: move, see the space between two players, and make sure that you can be seen between two players.

53

THRU BALLS

- Field of 33 yds. x 44 yds., 4 cones
- 2 teams of 4 players
- 5 x 3 minutes - 2 minutes active recovery

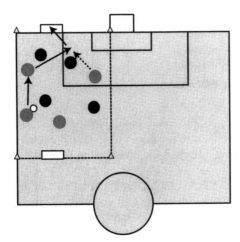

A goal may only be scored whenever the last pass is given between two opponents or one opponent and one of the outside lines of the field.

Objectives:
- Look for passes between two opponents.
- Ask for the ball at the proper moment.

Variations:
- Goals where the last pass was a cross played backwards between two opponents counts for three.
- Goals that are scored after a thru ball count double.
- A point is scored every time a thru ball is successful.

Commentary:
The teammate must be moving and ask for the ball in order for the pass between two opponents to occur. Teammates must be focused on asking for the ball.
50% of thru balls as the last pass lead to goals.

REACHING THE STRIKERS IN THE FREE SPACE

* Full field, 4 cones
* 2 teams of 8 to 10 players and 2 keepers
* 2 x 15 minutes - 2 minutes recovery

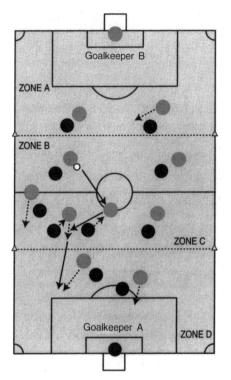

Every team has 2 strikers available in zones A and D.
Team B must attempt to hold the ball as long as possible in the middle of the field (zones B and C) in order to reach their strikers in zone D.

Team A applies high pressure in order to halt the progression of team B. Whenever team A wins the ball back, they look to break out quickly. The attackers look for the free space.

Objectives:
Keeping possession of the ball and looking for the free space.

Variation:
Allow one, then two players to enter the defensive zone.

PASS IN THE FREE SPACE

- Entire field, 4 cones
- 2 teams of 6 to 8 players and 2 goalkeepers

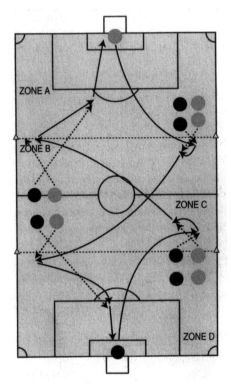

After a player changes positions, he receives the ball from the goalkeeper (throw). He then plays the ball short to a teammate who plays a long ball to a player on the other side of the middle line who has taken up a position there.

During the build-up the players make crossing runs at the middle line, resulting in the ability to receive the long pass.

The action is ended with a shot on goal.

This exercise can be performed on both sides of the field at the same time.

The players follow the ball after every pass.

Objective:
Look for the free space by means of the long ball.

PENETRATION:
THE PATH TO THE GOAL

The build-up of play, or to put it a better way, the penetration toward the opponents' distant goal, takes place in a well thought out manner.
There is a relationship between the use of the zones of the field and the path to the goal.

The penetration of the opponent's defensive line applies to the attacking strategy of a team specifically by:
* by-passing the defense
* penetrating the center of the defense by making a hole in the heart of the defensive position

The efficiency of each strategy (chapter Finishing the Attack) is about the same: 30% of goals are scored out of short passes, individual actions in front of the goal; and 30% are scored out of crosses, shifting the play, and long balls. On the basis of our findings, a general model with regards to penetration was conceived as follows:

PENETRATION MODELS

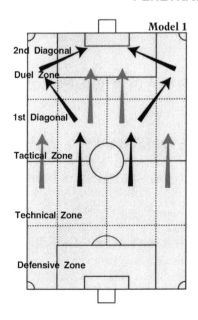

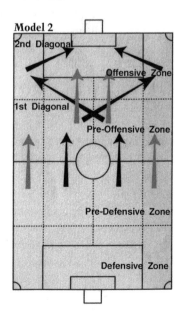

1 - HOW DO YOU GET TO THE OPPONENT'S GOAL?

In order to get to the opponents goal, the efficient team brings the ball in the pre-offensive zone (tactical zone) behind the second defensive line via one of the four lanes in the length and width, and is then prepared to approach:
• through first making use of a cross pass resulting in breaking open the defense, and getting in front of the goal by means of a second cross pass;
• through looking for an opening in the opponent's defense via an "wall-pass", 2 v 1, an individual action, or a pass splitting two players.

The choice between the two options depends upon the depth of the first action and the character of the defensive line.

A player will attempt to penetrate the opponent's defensive line if:
• it seems fragile, especially when:
        - the number of defenders is limited,
        - there is space between the lines,
• the defensive marking is man to man
• the attacker has already begun an individual action
• he has the chance to reach a teammate or work together with a teammate because he feels safe

The bypassing is prepared by the defense by means of placing cross passes (see penetration model) or through the switching of play in order to find the open player.

2 - HOW TO CHOOSE BETWEEN A DIRECTED AND A FAST ATTACK

In order to make a choice between these two types of attack, the player must win the ball and take into account:
• the position of the ball (offensive or defensive zone)
• the playable space (number of defenders in front of him)
• the positioning and movement of the defenders (position of the defenders)
• the position of the opponents, the number of opponents and the situation that he finds himself in.

3 - PRINCIPLE OF ATTACK AGAINST A STRENGTHENED DEFENSE

In order to attack against a strengthened defense, a team needs to:
* make free space
* make sure the attackers do not become pushed forward

MAKING FREE OFFENSIVE SPACE

The attackers are still moving in order to create free space (check back, ask diagonally, ...)

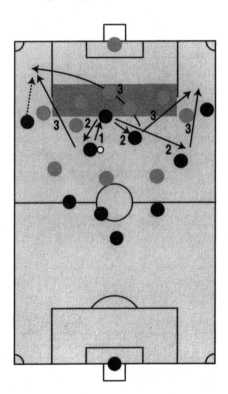

The midfielders and the defenders determine the play and coach the teammate who is standing with his back to the defense.

The forwards check back, while the midfielders move quickly into the free space.

After checking back, the forwards can:
* keep possession of the ball, turn and pass
* play the ball back on an angle to a midfielder (pass 2)
* lay the ball off to the side
* play the ball back on an angle (pass 3)

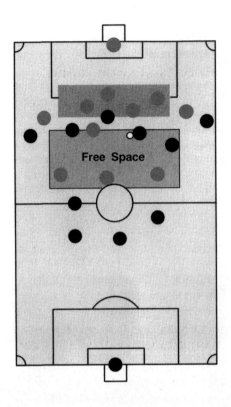

Free Space

WHY MUST THE MIDFIELDERS NOT PUSH UP ON THE FORWARDS?

If the attack runs up against a strengthened defense, the forwards must come out of the defensive wall, break free, switch and free up the space.

By following close to the forwards, the midfielders and defenders cling to the opponent's wall in the playable space of the opponent's defenders. Thus they leave the free space open behind them that the opponent can make use of.

The midfielders must consequently remain in their line and the forwards are required to play the ball back. From out of this they can quickly and briefly dive into the free space behind the defenders.

4 - COMMENTARY

By observing the top teams we have learned that:

Teams that win:
◆ make use of the entire width of the field and their positioning is more evenly balanced,
◆ start runs from farther away in the pre-offensive and pre-defensive zones,
◆ win the ball farther back in their own half,
◆ show better control bringing the ball through the opponent's half, "pushing it inside" via a minimum of two central paths.

Teams that lose:
• prefer to by-pass the defense,
• begin their penetrating runs in the opponent's zones.

This demonstrates that they have inadequate control over the ball and their tactics are more tuned to exploit mistakes by the opponent in the opponent's half.

5 - TRAINING:
EXERCISES AND GAME RELATED FORMS

The aim is to divide up the tasks and functions for every player on the field.
These tasks are related to the zones, paths and positions.

The lines that are visible on the field relate to the playing rules. But there are also invisible lines that the players must pick up in order perform the playing system well.

The splitting up of the field into different zones forms a virtual fact of the sport of soccer. How the players pick up these lines and zones is by utilizing them during the exercises and game related forms in the different zones of the field.
The player must consciously understand how the center of the field and the runs in the zones are related.

NOTE:
Do not hesitate to set down the virtual lines on the field or make use of the lines that are already there.

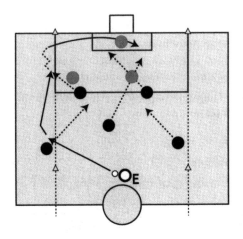

BY-PASS THE DEFENSE

* Half field, 4 cones
* 5 against 2 + 1 keeper

The coach starts the play.

One player positions himself on the right flank or on the left flank.
Ask for the ball on the flank, play the ball into space, cross the ball, make crossing runs.

Emphasis lies on the quality of the passes, the crosses and the runs of the attackers.

TARGET PLAYER - ONE TOUCH PASS

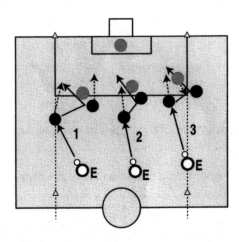

* Half field, 4 cones
* 3 situations, 2 against 1
* Each situation is played separately

The coach starts the play.

Pay attention to the target player that the defender is closely marking, and ask for a quick movement from the player when he receives the pass.

Emphasis lies on the criteria that need to be present in order for a wall-pass to be successful:
* assess the opponent,
* after the passes, acceleration from the player who asks for the ball

ONE - TWO - THREE

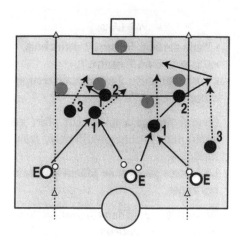

* Half field, 4 cones
* 2 situations 3 against 2 (situation in the center of the field, situation on the flank)

The coach starts play from different areas of the field.

One - two to play in the third player in the offensive zones (action 3) in the center of the field as well as over the flanks.

Emphasis lies on the quality of the call for the ball, determined by the offensive tactics (go to the outside or shoot).
In this exercise the strikers are asked to be creative.

BY-PASS THE DEFENSE: CROSSES

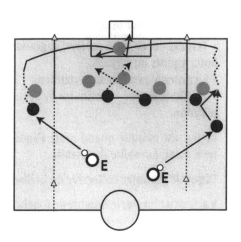

* Half field, 4 cones
* 1 against 1 on the left flank
* 2 against 1 on the right flank
* 2 against 3 in the central zone

The coach starts the play.
A goal is scored after a cross or a final pass.

Objectives:
* by-pass the defense and find the hole in the defense.
* create a situation of numerical superiority.
* strive for defensive organization and defenders supporting each other.

Variations: change the number of players on the flanks.
The attackers are required to make crossing runs. The players change positions with each other.

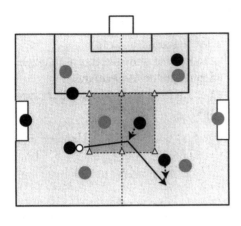

PENETRATION VIA THE TACTICAL ZONE

- Half field, 6 cones, 2 small goals
- 6 against 6 or 7 against 7
- 3 x 4 minutes - 2 minutes recovery

Every team has a supporting player in the pre-offensive zone (tactical zone).
The other players may not move into these zones.

Objectives: support in the tactical zone, space for the midfielders.

Variation: limit the number of ball contacts.

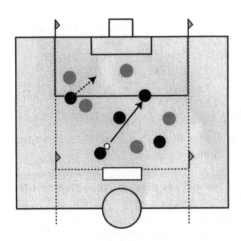

PENETRATION PER BLOCK

- Field of 44 yds. x 38 yds., 2 big goals, 4 cones or corner flags
- 5 against 5 with or without keepers
- 2 x 10 minutes - 2 minutes recovery

A goal counts only when the entire team is over the middle line.

Objective: move up-field as a team with the ball.

Variation: limit the number of ball contacts.

Commentary: do not award a goal if the entire team is not over the middle line. The emphasis lies with the team organization.

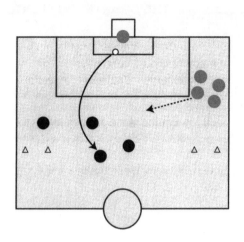

PENETRATION IN A POORLY POSITIONED DEFENSE

* Half field, 4 cones
* 2 teams of 4 or 5 players and 1 goalkeeper
* blocks of 15 seconds
* 6 x 3 minutes - 1 minute recovery

The goalkeeper throws the ball to the attacking team. The attackers attempt to score before defenders can get back into their positions. Whenever the defenders win the ball back, they try to dribble the ball through one of the two sets of goals. The coach whistles to mark the end of the action after 15 seconds, and begins the play again after 30 seconds. The players change roles after 3 minutes.

Objective: begin a fast attack against a poorly positioned defense.

Variations: all of the attackers must touch the ball. The play is over after 6 seconds and begins again in 15 seconds.

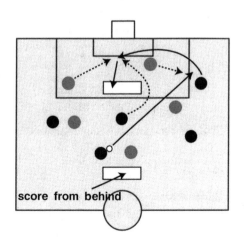

score from behind

PENETRATION OVER THE FLANKS

* Half field, 2 movable goals turned backwards
* 5 against 5 without keepers
* 5 x 3 minutes - 1 minute recovery

The players must go behind the goal in order to score.

Objective: penetration over the flanks.

Variation: score a goal by means of a volley or a head ball.

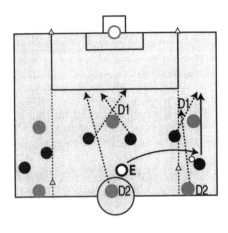

PENETRATION BY MEANS OF THE COUNTER ATTACK

* Half field, 4 cones
* 6 defenders and 1 keeper against 6 attackers
* 3 playing zones with 2 attackers against 1 defender
* 2 x 12 minutes - 1 minute recovery

Out of a 2 v 1 situation the attackers attempt to put the defenders into trouble by passing to the striker in the middle zone.

The coach begins the play along one flank, and then along the other flank.

The two defenders, D2, who stand behind the middle line, move in to help their teammates and force 2 v 2 situations. The play switches from over the right flank to over the left flank.

Objective: fast attack in numerical superiority.

Variation: the defenders leave from behind the goal.

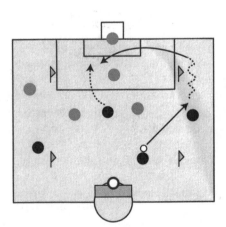

AROUND THE OUTSIDE: GIVING CROSSES

* Half field, 4 corner flags
* 4 against 4 with or without a goalkeeper
* 3 x 4 minutes - 2 minutes recovery

A goal is awarded if the ball is played wide of the flag that results in a cross.

Objective: score after a cross.

Variations: limit the number of passes. Score a goal from a head ball or by means of a volley or half volley.

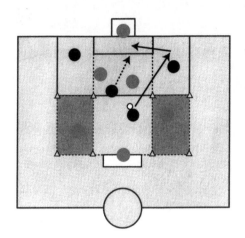

MAKING USE OF SUPPORTING PLAYERS IN THE ZONES

* Half field, 8 cones
* 2 against 2 with or without a keeper + 2 supporting players in the zones
* 3 x 4 minutes - 2 minutes recovery

A goal is awarded whenever it results from a cross given from a supporting player who is in one of the zones.

The supporting players remain in the zones.

Objective: scoring after a cross.

Variation: limit the number of passes.

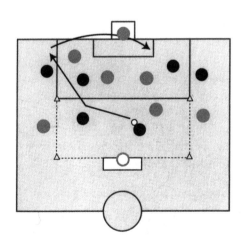

MAKING USE OF SUPPORTING PLAYERS IN THE ZONES

* Half field, 4 cones
* 3 against 3 with or without a keeper + 2 support players
* 3 x 4 minutes - 2 minutes recovery

A goal is awarded whenever it came from a cross given from a supporting player who is in one of the zones.
The supporting players may take part in the play.

Objective: scoring after a cross.

Variation: limit the number of passes.

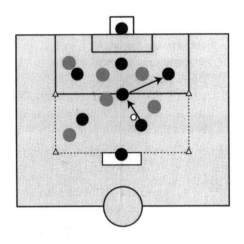

TRANSITION TO A FAST ATTACK

• Field of 44 yds. x 33 yds., 2 goals, 4 cones
• 6 against 6 with keeper
• 3 x 3 minutes - 2 minutes recovery

As soon as a team loses possession of the ball, all of that team's players must first leave the field via the sidelines before they may continue on with the game.

Objectives:
• scoring against a poorly positioned defense.
• change over to a fast attack.
• training the goalkeepers.

Commentary: This is a tiring game. Adjust the number of players as needed for the game.

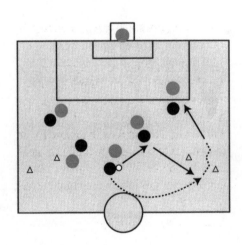

PENETRATION VIA THE FLANKS

• Half field, 4 cones
• 5 against 5
• 5 x 3 minutes - 1 minute recovery

It is required to play over the flanks through the gates marked by the cones.

Objective: dismantle the defense.

Variation: limit the number of ball contacts.

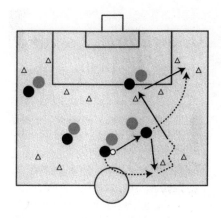

PENETRATION VIA THE WINGS AND THE CENTER

• Half field, 12 cones
• 3 teams of 5 players
• 5 against 5
• change the team after about 3 minutes
• 5 x 3 minutes - 3 minutes recovery

It is required to dribble or pass through the gateways marked by the cones.

Objective: choose the best situation to push through the defense.

Variation: limit the number of ball contacts.

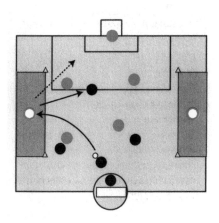

PENETRATE VIA THE FLANKS WITH SUPPORTING PLAYERS

• Half field, 4 cones
• 5 against 5 with goalkeepers + 2 neutral players
• 5 x 3 minutes - 1 minute recovery

The goalkeepers begin the play. The two neutral players who stand on the flanks (gray zones) play with the team in possession of the ball. As long as they do not receive the ball, they may not leave the zone. They may not attack as long as they have not received the ball. As soon as a neutral player has received the ball, he takes part in the play. As soon as the ball is lost, the neutral players quickly move back into the zones so that they other team may use them.

Objectives: make use of the flanks and strive for a numerical advantage in the attack.

Variations: limit the number of ball contacts. Switch to make use of both flanks.

PENETRATION AFTER A DRIBBLE

- Half field, 4 cones
- 5 against 5 + 1 keeper
- 5 x 3 minutes - 1 minute recovery

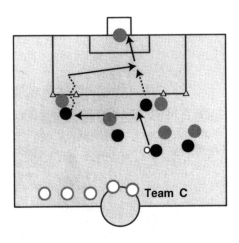

In order to make the attackers familiar with going over the flanks, they are required to go through the gates on both sides of the top of the 18-yard box.

If they are successful in dribbling through the gate, they may cross the ball or shoot on goal.

If the defenders win the ball back, they play the ball out over the flanks.

Objectives:
- By-pass the defense.
- Shift the play.
- Offensive dribble.

Variation:
If the defenders win the ball back, they play the ball to team C standing in the center circle.

Commentary:
The exercise is successful whenever the attackers instinctively switch the play to the "open" side.

MAKING USE OF THE FLANKS

- Full field, 6 cones
- 11 against 11 with goalkeepers
- 4 x 7 minutes - 1 minute recovery

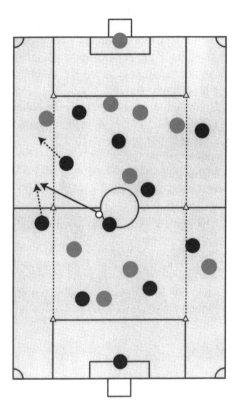

A goal is scored by taking a specific number of ball contacts in the different zones.

Limit the number of ball contacts in all of the zones in their own half.
In the opponent's half:
- in the middle zone: one touch
- in the outside zone: two touches
- in the penalty area: unlimited touches

Objective:
Organize the ball circulation in the different zones of the field.

Variations:
- Outside zone: free play
- Begin in an outside zone, end in another zone.
- Switch zones at least two times.

Commentary:
The players are required to make use of cross passes. The use of the zones becomes self-evident.

GOING AROUND - MAKING USE OF THE FLANKS AND CROSS PASSES

- Full field, 6 cones
- 11 against 11 with goalkeepers
- 4 x 8 minutes - 1 minute recovery

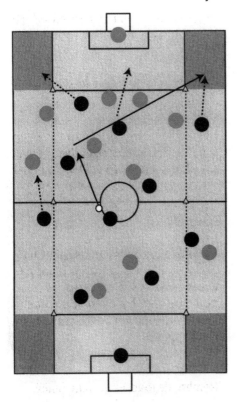

The defenders may not enter the gray zones. So, these zones are free for the attackers

Objectives:
- Penetration via the flanks.
- Make use of cross passes.

Variations:
- Limit the number of ball contacts depending upon the zones.
- Switch zones at least twice.

Commentary:
The players are required to make cross passes; making use of the flanks is self-evident.

PENETRATION - ATTEMPTING TO SPREAD THE DEFENSE OUT

* A reduced full field, 4 cones
* 9 against 7 (among which 1 is a goalkeeper)
* 4 x 7 minutes - 2 minutes recovery

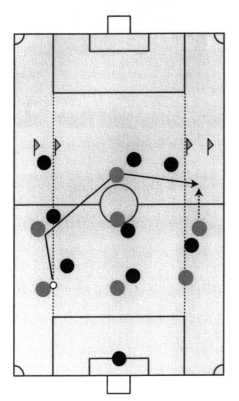

Short build-up through the goalkeeper or through a throw-in.

The team that defends the small goals attempts to score in the big goal by making use of its numerical superiority.

The team that defends the big goal must attempt to collectively keep the ball by moving up as a block and spreading out the opponents in order to score in the small goals.

Objectives:
* Collectively keep possession of the ball in order to allow the block to push up into the middle zone, and then switch the play.
* Defend far from own goal at a numerical disadvantage along the flank by leaving the other far zone free.

Variations:
* Limit the number of ball contacts.
* Switch the ball to the other side in order to score.
* Begin along one side and end along the other side.

BUILD-UP OVER THE FLANKS

- a reduced full field between both penalty areas, 2 corner flags
- 10 against 10 with keepers
- 4 x 7 minutes - 2 minutes recovery

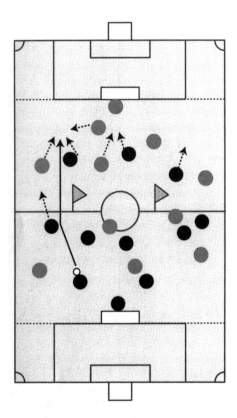

Between the two flags is an off limits zone:
- for the ball
- for the player in possession of the ball

Objectives:
- Direct the play toward the flanks.
- Penetrate over the flanks.

Variations:
- Limit the number of ball contacts.
- Players remain in their zone.

PENETRATE UP THE MIDDLE

- ◆ A reduced full field between both penalty areas, 2 corner flags
- ◆ 10 against 10 with keepers
- ◆ 4 x 7 minutes - 2 minutes recovery

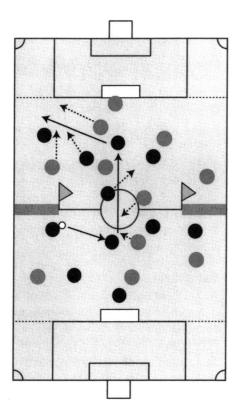

The zones between the flags and the and the sidelines (gray zones) are forbidden:
- ◆ for the ball
- ◆ for the player in possession of the ball

Objectives:
- ◆ Making it mandatory to cross the advantage line and attempt to play the ball as quickly as possible into the opponent's half.
- ◆ Learn to make choices: attack up the middle or by-pass the defense.

Variations:
- ◆ As soon as the ball is in the opponent's half, look to the sides to by-pass the defenders.
- ◆ Playing through the middle.
- ◆ Limit the number of ball contacts.

DIRECT ATTACK < - - > FAST ATTACK

• Full field, 2 cones
• 2 against 2 + 1 keeper B in zone 1
• 8 against 8 + 1 keeper A in zone 2
• 4 x 7 minutes - 2 minutes recovery

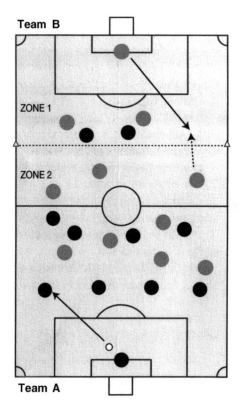

The keeper from team A plays in a flank defender. The keeper from team B plays in a defender that checks back to the ball.

Objectives:
• Team A attempts to keep possession of the ball until finally playing in the two strikers under favorable circumstances.
• Team B applies high pressure in order to win possession.

Variations:
• Allow two more on-rushing attackers to enter zone 1 in order for the offensive team to gain a numerical advantage.
• Allow a supporting defender to come back into the defensive zone (zone 1).

ADJUSTMENT OF THE ATTACK AS IT RELATES TO THE DEFENSIVE POSITIONING

* Full field
* Zone 1: 3 against 2 + 1 keeper
* Zone 2: 5 against 4 + 1 keeper
* 4 x 8 minutes - 2 minutes recovery

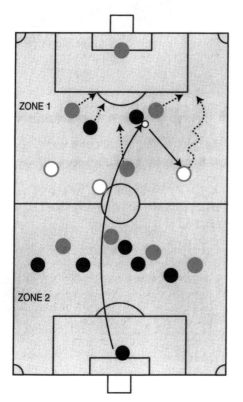

Three neutral players switch play in zones 1 and 2.

The play begins from the goalkeepers or the coach who play in the forwards or a running defender.

With every attack, two of the neutral players out of the midfield join the attackers while one neutral player remains behind to support the build-up as needed.

Objectives:
* The manner of the attack is adjusted depending upon the positioning of the defense.
* Defending in a numerical disadvantage situation (counter attack).

Variation:
* Limit the number of ball contacts.

ADJUSTING THE PLAY IN RELATION TO THE SITUATION IN THE ATTACK AND IN THE DEFENSE

- Full field, 4 cones
- 3 against 2 in zone 1
- 5 against 5 in zone 2 and in zone 3
- 2 against 3 in zone 4
- 4 x 8 minutes - 2 minutes recovery

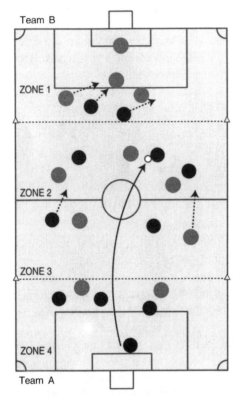

A long kick by the goalkeeper. Win the ball in the middle zone, then ball circulation followed by a situation in the finishing zone.

Objective:
The play adjusts in relation to the different situations in the attack and defense.

Variations:
- A numerical disadvantage in the attacking aspect.
- A numerical advantage in the attacking aspect.

Commentary:
Win the duels with the ball in zone 2.

78

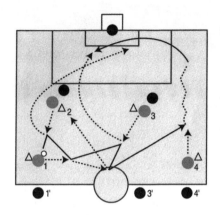

TRAINING SWITCHING THE FIELD

◆ Half field, 4 cones that mark the positions of the players
◆ 2 defenders + 1 keeper
◆ 4 attackers
◆ 20 minutes with changing of the defenders about every 5 minutes

The outside left player looks for support from the left striker, then combines with the right striker to play in the right midfielder, who pushes up to send in a cross in front of the goal. The two strikers make crossing runs.

Objective: begin an action on one flank - end it on the other flank.

Variations: the coach determines the degree of pressure from the two defenders. The same exercise played over the left side.

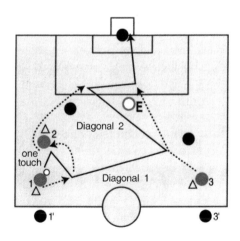

PENETRATION WITH 2 PLAYERS AND A TARGET PLAYER

◆ Half field, 3 cones that mark the positions of the players
◆ 3 attackers and 2 defenders + 1 keeper
◆ 2 x 10 minutes, change the defenders after 5 minutes

The left midfielder plays the ball to the left striker who plays the ball one touch. This is followed by a cross pass to the right midfielder.

Objective: one touch and cross passes through the center of the field.

Variations: pressure from defenders. The same exercise on the right side.

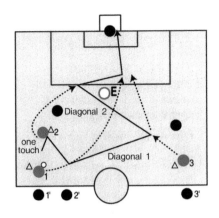

PENETRATION WITH 3 PLAYERS

* Half field
* 3 cones that mark the positions of the players
* 3 attackers and 2 defenders + 1 goalkeeper
* 2 x 10 minutes, defenders change after 5 minutes

After one touch passing with the target player 2 and after a diagonal pass or a cross pass, player 1 carries his action further and makes a crossing run with player 3.

Objective: strive for diagonal passes and crossing runs; carry out the actions until the very end.

Commentary: the emphasis lies on the fluidness of the passes and the positioning.

Variation: the same exercise on the left side.

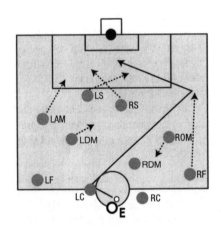

OFFENSIVE PHASE: SWITCHING PLACES

* Half field. Work with figures or cones in order to give the start positions. The entire team without opponents.
* Work in short sequences
* Two times along each side
* Not systemizing
* Changing of positions between the ROM and the RF

Objective: fluidity in the passes and movements during the changing of positions.

Variations: switching of positions between the ROM and the RF and between the midfielders ROM and RDM. Changing of positions between ROM and LS who asks for the deep pass.

LEGEND

LS: left striker	RDM: right defensive midfielder
RS: right striker	LF: left flank defender
LAM: left attacking midfielder	RF: right flank defender
ROM: right offensive midfielder	LC: left central defender
LDM: left defensive midfielder	RC: right central defender

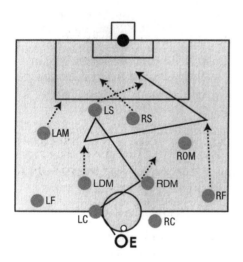

OFFENSIVE PHASE: LOOKING FOR THE DEEP PASS

◆ Half field. The entire team without opposition
◆ Working along both sides
◆ Looking for a midfielder, which leads to giving the deep pass.

Objective: fluidity in the passes and movements while looking for the target for the deep pass.

Variations: first pass is wide for the flank defender who plays the deep pass. Limit the number of ball contacts.

ORGANIZATION: THE POSITIONING OF THE PLAYERS

The game organization forms the basis for the behavior of the players. It determines the roles on the field, with an eye on obtaining the most efficiency for the whole. It is self evident that a team cannot play without a collective organization.

The actions of every player are made in relation to the others. Their tactical insight allows them to apply it to game situations in order to solve them for the good of the team.

The playing organization (*strategy*) is constantly in motion. The elements are still changing and the improvement of technique, physique, and the tactical level of the players brings about changes.

The playing organization adjusts itself. The team organizes itself in relation to the determining elements, by taking into account its own merits (*qualities and weaknesses*) as well as those of the opponent. The team intuitively plays to its strong points and hides its weak points. The coach tries to recognize the qualities and weaknesses of his team and as a result improve upon the weak points and maintain the strong ones to raise the level of the team.

The game organization is permanent while the game plan (*tactics*) is of a temporary nature and is related to one single match. For the player, it is identical to a situation.

"The system gives security whenever things are not going so well. It makes it possible to explode whenever everything is going well. Whenever the block is held and the distance between the lines is observed, there is no danger. By reducing the space it gives a chance for more offensive players in regards to bringing creativity." (Elie Baup)

"The intention is to be as organized as possible in order to win the ball back with the least amount of effort." (Claude Puel)

From a very good organization one expects:
• that the entire width of the field is well occupied
• that the space between the opposing players is occupied in order to prevent them from pushing up
• that the opponent must run

• that the physical effort, the running effort, is reduced
• that they can easily get in front of the opponent's goal

In order to respond to this assumption, modern soccer has developed the concept of the "team block", and has coupled an organizational system to this block. The integration of these concepts with the players takes a substantial amount of work during the training sessions.

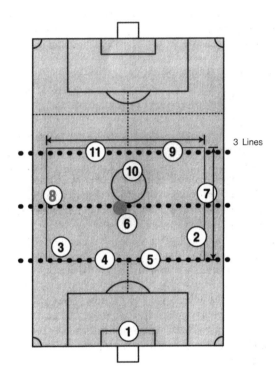

3 Lines

THE "TEAM BLOCK"

• The "team block", or "block" for short, is determined by a rectangle from which the sides are specified by the players who are positioned closest to the center of the field.

• Observations show that winning teams have a block that is measurably smaller than teams that lose.
The distance between the players is limited.

1 - THE ORGANIZATION

A - THE PLAYING SYSTEM

The qualities of the players determine the organizational form that enables them to perform as well as possible. The wise use of players on the field determines the position, the placement on the field and the position in the play in relation to the tactical situation.

The systems of play that at this moment are employed the most are the 4-4-2, 4-3-3, and the 3-5-2.
Complete individual man-marking is a thing of the past.

For the average team playing with three defenders, whereby the two flank players push up in the midfield, it is more difficult than playing with four defenders.

In the middle, teams with one single defender are passed by and do not find a balance. The speed of the counter attack requires at least two players in that part of the game. The teams no longer leave the flanks free since these have become important for attacking play.

There are many offensive formations but the greatest number of teams utilize a 4-4-2 with two centrally positioned players.

The availability of multifaceted players in offensive positions is a considerable advantage because the play is thus less predictable for the opponent.

Some teams make use of three forwards, but usually two forwards who are either next to each other or one behind the other are used.

B - THE TACTICAL STARTING POINT OF PLAY

1 - THE DEFENSIVE STARTING POINT

The constant searching for a playing structure makes it possible to put the player in a position to once again win the ball back.

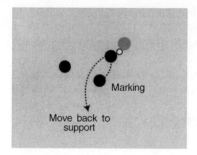

INDIVIDUAL PRINCIPLES

The value of the defender is determined by his choices and by supporting his teammates and being helped by their marking so he gets back in the block (once again taking up positions in the coverage).

COLLECTIVE PRINCIPLES

The purpose consists of throwing up a defensive dam in front of the

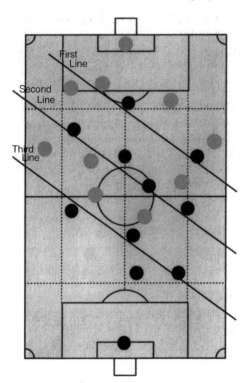

opponent in possession of the ball with players who are consistently moving.

This dam relies on the organizational lines: the forwards, midfielders and the defenders.

The first line serves to delay the opponent's attack, the second line is the hunting- and interception zone, the third forms the relief line from the opponent's attack. The density of players that populate every line depends upon the system that is decided on by the coach.

In the dynamic phase these lines are reduced to two.

It is important that every player is aware that the formation is constantly in motion and that it must be constantly adjusted. The formation changes in relation to the movement of the ball, of the positioning of the opponents and of the distribution of players between the lines.

The collective defensive effort has everything to do with erecting a permanent dam from the three lines. The players who make up a part of every line direct their running path toward the player with the ball resulting in him not being able to play a forward pass.

The predominant collective principles are: zone defending, individual defending, mixed defending, and line defending.

2 - THE OFFENSIVE STARTING POINT

By this it is understood the striving for penetration by the player in possession of the ball to advance toward the opponent's goal. This endeavor is dependent upon the position and formation of the opponents. The player in possession of the ball must have the choice of the most efficient solution between the ones his teammates present him.

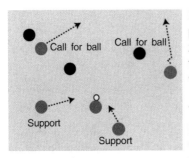

In order to advance the ball the player in possession must avoid the very crowded zones and look for a teammate who is the most suitable to bring the ball forward.

Thus the teammates must take up a position to ask for the ball either in front of the ball, in support on the flank, or in support behind the ball.

These tactical movements occur in motion, at a suitable moment by means of a pass.

C - DIFFERENT DEFENSIVE ORGANIZATIONS

1 - MARKING

Marking an opponent entails all of the arrangements that affect the interrupting of his actions at every moment within the boundaries of what is allowable under the rules of play.

The defender who is doing the marking must keep the following rules in mind:

* be constantly alert, especially when the ball is far away,
* constantly be a physical force when in the presence of an opponent,
* impose a moral presence,

* position yourself between the opponent and the goal,
* intercept the ball when the chance presents itself,
* do not rush head-long into an action without support,
* always keep open the possibility of intervention, do not allow yourself to be completely cut off from the play.

THE MARKING CAN TAKE ON THE FOLLOWING FORMS

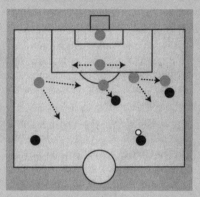

* complete: the defender is ready to intervene as soon as an opponent comes near;
* controlling: whenever the ball is far away, the defender watches his direct opponent while giving support to his teammates, "be observant";
* supporting: the defender stands diagonally behind (supporting) in relation to a teammate who can intervene if necessary;
* take over position: the defender moves into the position of an out-played teammate;
* drop-off: the defender drops off the opponent in order to win the ball back;
* delay: the defender drops off gradually in front of an opponent in order to make a collective regrouping possible.

---

2 - ZONE DEFENDING

This type of defending is made up of a defensive block set up to remain between the ball and the goal. The field is arranged into virtual zones. The players occupy the zones and intervene as soon as the ball enters their zone. They defend by watching the opponent and marking individually within their respective zones. The closer to the goal, the closer the marking becomes.

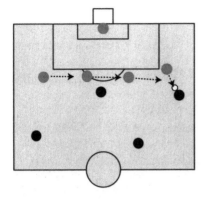

The organization always shows ladder effect lines by which the closest to the ball starts a combination. The other lines give support.
The players are positioned in relation to the ball and the goal. Their positioning changes while the support takes place in relation to the movement of the ball. As soon as a line is played through, a new line offers resistance to the progression of the ball and once again attempts to win it back.

Zone defending protects the path to the goal and makes if difficult for the opponent to advance to the goal. The individual shortcomings of a player are made up for. It makes interception possible, because the player who takes the action knows that he has support. It is much easier to build up through the great number of options as soon as the ball is won back.

The opponent nevertheless holds the initiative; his efficiency is profitable only in limited zones. This brings a certain passivity to the players who are farther from the ball. It requires constant liveliness from all of the players and benefits anticipation.

3 - MIXED DEFENDING

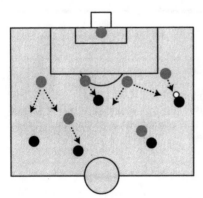

Mixed defending combines the advantages of individual defending and zone defending.

Every player plays in a zone and watches an opponent who enters that zone.
In his zone the defender concerns himself first and foremost with the winning back of the ball and then ensures the build-up.

The supporting of teammates takes place in zones in order to strive for a numerical advantage in the defense.

This type of defending judges the value of he defender by allowing him to take the initiative to make choices.

4 - LINE DEFENDING

The recovery of the ball relies on putting the opposing attackers into an offside position. As soon as the ball is brought into play, the defenders quickly move forward toward the middle and position themselves in relation to the central attackers.

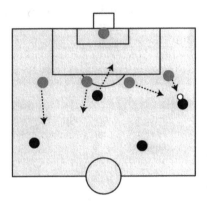

Line defending requires concentration, watchfulness and teamwork between all of the defenders: the movement of one defender brings about the movement of the other defenders as well.

Line defending is only efficient whenever the defenders react with the same automation. It is vulnerable whenever the attackers are proficient dribblers, play one-two combinations and whenever a player comes up from behind the play. It is a means to combat a direct playing style.

How can the coach make a choice between these defensive types?

The choice of a collective defensive organization depends upon:
• the attitude of the defenders, their aggressiveness,
• the choice of players,
• the quality of the players,
• the objective: get a result, try to build-up.

D - OFFENSIVE ORGANIZATION

The collective organization of the attack includes the entire team, but especially the forwards and midfielders.
The midfielders contribute to the development of the action. The forwards' task is to finish it.

ORGANIZATION WITH 2 FORWARDS

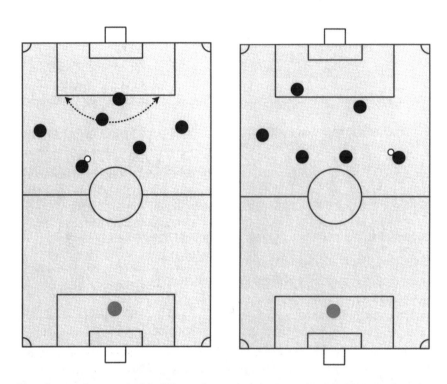

Two forwards, one behind the other: the deepest forward keeps the defense busy and attempts to tear the block open; the second roams around and makes use of the openings.

Two forwards in one line: combined movements of the two forwards: one moves to the side where the ball is, and the other in the free space.

One striker is necessary in the center because he represents an anchor-point. Whenever he stands with his back to the defense, he can come back through the defense into the free space.

ORGANIZATION WITH 3 FORWARDS

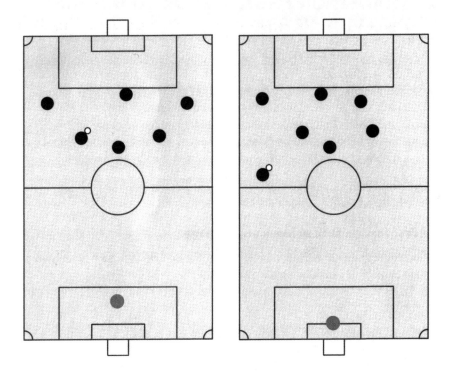

One central forward in an advanced position. The two others are positioned more behind, either as midfielders or as wing forwards.

Depending on their position in the formation, the midfielders carry the weight with the build-up through the central zones. The two flank defenders carry the ball in the zones if they take part in the attack. In this case the flank forward comes to the aid of the flank defender.

2 - TRANSITION FROM ATTACK TO DEFENSE AND VICE VERSA

A - TRANSITION FROM DEFENSIVE TO ATTACKING POSITIONING

WINNING BACK THE BALL WITH A DISORGANIZED OPPOSITION DEFENSE

Bring the ball as quickly as possible in front of the opponent's goal:
• by an individual action that leads to the ball quickly moving into the free space
• by a long pass in the depth for a teammate who has slipped into the free space.

The team pushes up quickly in order to gain a numerical advantage, take up positions in the free space, and support teammates.

WINNING THE BALL BACK WITH AN ORGANIZED OPPOSITION DEFENSE

The ball circulation must be well controlled resulting in unbalancing the defense and by-passing it. Thus one must:
• keep the play wide over the flanks, lure the defenders out away from their required zone in order to weaken the defense in front of the goal,
• ask for the ball in the free space. The last pass must put the attacker in a shooting position. This phase must happen quickly with a changing of the rhythm.

B - TRANSITION FROM ATTACKING TO DEFENSIVE POSITIONING

The opponent won the ball back from a disorganized defense.
The intention is:
• to delay the progression of the ball without allowing it to get free (zone pressing),
• to reform the defensive line, filling in the vacant positions without worrying about their role in the organization.

The opponent wins the ball back from an organized defense.
The team must retake possession of the ball, either through an individual action or through a collective action.

Aim:
* allow the player in possession to attack through the player in the zone
* strive to gain a numerical advantage in the defense (cover, dropping back in support)
* reduce the free space

3 - THE POSITIONING OF THE PLAYERS

"I was often told that a soccer player must not run with the ball, but that the ball must do the work. In fact it comes down to it that the block must push forward in possession of the ball; the opponent must thus run after what is the basis of soccer: the ball". (J. Cruyff)

On the field the players position themselves in order to attack or to defend. The positioning in the attacking aspect includes the asking for the ball (positioning towards the goal) and giving support (positioning towards the ball). Positioning in the defensive aspect includes giving cover and taking up a new position (coming back). The proportion of this positioning is different for every player depending on his position. Playing in front is, after all, not the same as playing in the back. The geometry of the actions in each position is different.

	FORWARDS	MIDFIELDERS	DEFENDERS
ATTACKING POSITIONING	65%	51%	38%
DEFENSIVE POSITIONING	35%	49%	62%

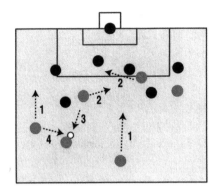

OBSERVATIONS GIVING THE FOUR BASIC POSITIONAL CHOICES:
* 1 - Ask for the ball while running toward the goal
* 2 - Ask for the ball at a diagonal to the goal
* 3 - Support from a player who is in front of the ball
* 4 - Support from a player who is positioned on the side

The whole animation problem lies in the runs and making good passes, one after the other.

4 - COMMENTARY

The efficiency of a team begins with a stable basic organization, which the players understand and accept. Naturally, an organization can never be the star; it must be applied and takes its form through the players themselves in relation to the match.
In "modern" soccer, improvisation is frowned upon, the players are acquainted with how far they may go and their role. The big competitions prove this.

In 2002, the most used playing systems were the 4 - 4 - 2 and the 3 - 5 - 2. However, every coach must choose a system that fits with the abilities of his players resulting in having a compact block from which the central point is found behind the middle line.

From our observations we have concluded that the block of winning teams:
* is positioned more on the left side;
* is shorter and more compact with less of a difference between maximum and minimum,
* has a center point that can be found just under the middle line

5 - TRAINING:
EXERCISES AND GAME RELATED FORMS

A - TACTICAL EXERCISES

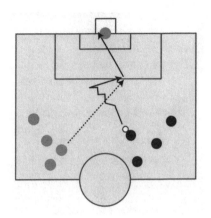

CROSSING RUNS BEHIND THE PLAYER IN POSSESSION OF THE BALL

* Half field
* 2 groups of 4 to 6 players + 1 keeper

Pass in front of the player who dives behind him.
Crossing run behind the second player who brings the ball under control and finishes.

Emphasis lies in the run and the receiving of information, while bringing the ball under control, by the player who receives it.

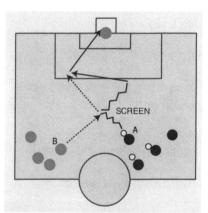

SCREEN

* Half field
* 2 groups of 4 to 6 players + 1 keeper

After dribbling the ball, player A provides a screen, leaves the ball for B, then continues his run diagonally where he then receives the ball again and finishes on goal.

Emphasis lies on the run and receiving of information during the run, and on the quality of the ball control.

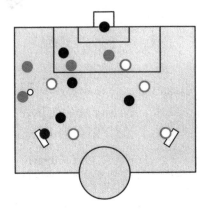

ATTACK - DEFENDING WITH CHOICES OF THE SIDES

• Half field, three goals
• 3 teams of 5 players without keepers
• 3 x 4 minutes - 2 minutes recovery

Every team defends their goal and attacks the other two goals.

Objective: transition from defending in a numerical advantage to attacking at a numerical disadvantage.
Variations: insert a neutral player who joins the team in possession of the ball. The neutral player may not by attacked by a defender.
Commentary: check on the player's insight into the game.

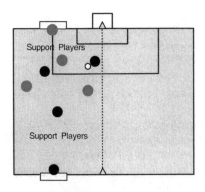

ATTACKING ANIMATION: GIVING SUPPORT

• Quarter field, 2 cones
• 2 against 2 = 2 permanent support players with goalkeepers
• 3 x 3 minutes - 2 minutes recovery

The support player may not attack or defend, he may only pass.

Objective: make use of the support players.
Variation: play with one touch.
Commentary: emphasis lies on the availability of the players and the positioning.

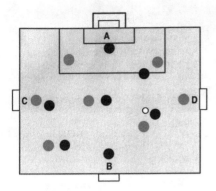

ATTACK - DEFENDING: TAKING UP POSITIONS QUICKLY

* Half field, 4 small goals
* 7 against 7 without goalkeepers
* 3 x 3 minutes - 2 minutes active recovery

Team 1 attacks goals C and D.
Team 2 attacks goals A and B.

Objectives: as soon as the ball is won back, the players must very quickly take up new positions in an attacking situation against two goals.
Improve the insight into the game.

Variation: play two touch.

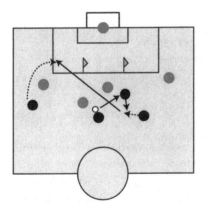

PUT UP A FIGHT AGAINST A STRENGTHENED DEFENSE

* Half field, 2 cones or corner flags
* 4 against 4 + 1 keeper
* 4 x 3 minutes - 1 minute recovery

The players may not go through the gate.

The team in possession must score a goal without their players going through the gate.

Objective: playing against a strengthened defense.

Variations: the ball may not be played through the gate. Increase the number of attackers.

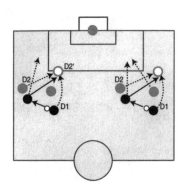

HOW DO YOU PLAY AGAINST A WALL-PASS?

* Quarter field
* 2 against 2 defenders D1 and D2
* 2 types of wall-passes

Objective: with the attempting of a wall-pass, the defenders anticipate the second pass.

Defender D2 quickly moves to position D2'.

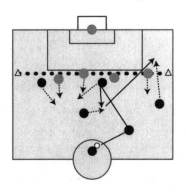

HOW DO YOU BREAK THROUGH A LINE DEFENSE?

* Half field, 2 cones
* 6 against 4 + 1 goalkeeper
* 5 x 4 minutes - 2 minutes recovery

The coach starts the play from out of the center circle.
The defenders play as a line defense. The attackers must search for a solution.

Objective:
Break through the line defense.

Commentary:
Emphasis lies on the fact that when the forwards drop back the defenders follow. The midfielders are asked to find solutions without crowding the forwards.

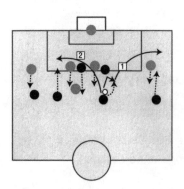

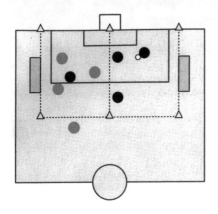

TRANSITION FROM ATTACKING TO DEFENDING

◆ Field of 50 yds. x 28 yds., 2 small goals, 6 cones
◆ 4 against 4 and 1 neutral player
◆ 5 x 3 minutes - 2 minutes recovery

Whenever a team intercepts the ball, the neutral player comes into play. Whenever a team loses the ball, the neutral player leaves the play.

Objective: quickly transition from attacking to defending and visa versa.

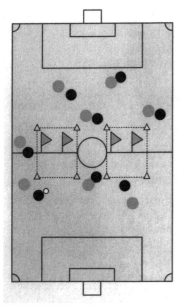

EVERYONE ATTACKS, EVERYONE DEFENDS

◆ Field between the penalty areas, 8 cones and 4 corner flags
◆ 8 against 8 with or without goalkeepers
◆ 4 x 5 minutes - 2 minutes recovery

The two teams score in two goals, from both sides:
Play with one touch in the marked off areas, three touch outside of the areas. A goal cannot be scored from an intercepted pass.
All players attack, all players defend.

Objective: keep moving in order to score a goal.

Variation: put a keeper in the goals.

Commentary: the rhythm of play is high. In order to guarantee progression in the play, it is better to begin with a single goal that is placed in the center circle.

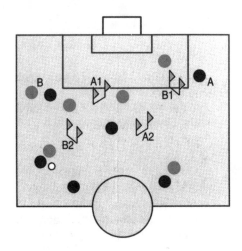

ATTACKING - DEFENDING

• Half field, 8 corner flags or cones
• 4 against 4 to 6 against 6
• 3 x 10 minutes - 2 minutes recovery

Team A scores in the two outside goals B1 and B2.
Team B scores by putting the ball through the central cones A1 and A2.
Change goals after every period.

Objectives: see things quickly and make the correct play. Learn to see the play more quickly.

Commentary: the rhythm is high and the game is interesting.

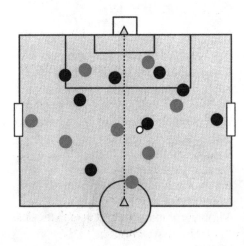

SEARCHING FOR THE OPEN PLAYER

• Half field, 2 goals on the sides, 2 cones
• 8 against 8
• 3 x 10 minutes - 2 minutes recovery

The players play normally, but they may not cross the middle line with the ball at their feet.

Objectives: look for the open player.

Commentary: this game forces the players to pick their head up and look ahead.

B - PLAY IN ZONES

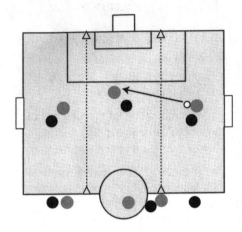

MARKING - GETTING OPEN

• Half field, 3 zones, 2 goals on the sides, 4 cones
• 1 against 1 in every zone
• 2 teams of 6 players
• 4 x 3 minutes - 1 min. 30 sec. active recovery

Objectives: the game is played at the maximum intensity and mobility of the players. The player breaks free of his mark and asks for the ball in space.

Variations: the defender or attacker may change zones. No more than two players per zone. The ball can not be played over the middle zone.

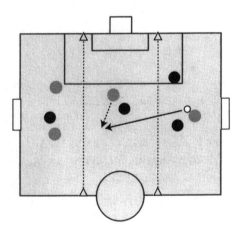

MOVEMENT - AGILITY

• Half field, 3 zones, 2 goals on the sides, 4 cones
• 2 forwards - 1 midfielder - 1 defender per team
• 4 x 3 minutes - 1 min. 30 sec. recovery (stretching)

The players do not change zones.
The forwards must score without being offside.

Objectives: the game is played at the maximum intensity and mobility of the players. Defend against two forwards. Attack at a numerical advantage.

Variations: the midfielder may change zones in order to help the defender or the forwards. The ball can not be played over the middle zone.

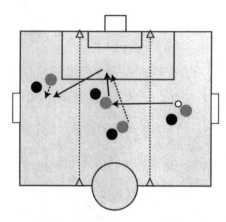

SUPPORT

♦ Half field, 3 zones, 2 goals on the sides, 4 cones
♦ 1 forward - 2 midfielders - 1 defender per team
♦ 4 x 3 minutes - 1 min. 30 sec. recovery (stretching)

The ball must be played to every zone.

Objectives: creating conditions for a perpetually open player, stimulate a changing of directions. Make use of the player in support. Prepare for a quick attack over the middle zone.

Variations: the midfielders may change zones in order to help the defender or attacker and to create a numerical advantage. The supporting player asks for the ball to create an offensive numerical advantage in another zone.

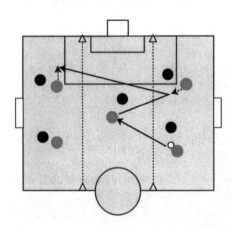

QUICKLY CHANGING FROM ONE ZONE TO ANOTHER

♦ Half field, 3 zones, 2 goals on the sides, 4 cones
♦ 2 forwards - 1 midfielder - 2 defenders per team
♦ 4 x 3 minutes - 1 min. 30 sec. recovery (stretching)

The ball must enter the middle zone before it can be played over the zone.

Objectives: give a deep pass after a ball that is laid off backwards. Quickly leave the defensive zone.

Variations: a player may change zones. Make use of cross passes.

INSIGHT INTO FREE SPACES

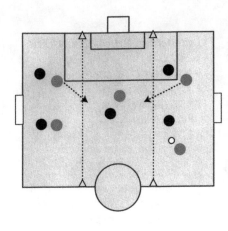

• Half field, 3 zones, 2 goals on the sides, 4 cones
• 5 against 5 or 6 against 6 with or without goalkeepers
• 4 x 3 minutes - 1 min. 30 sec. recovery (stretching)

The players are free to move about. The number of actions (pass, dribble, duel) is limited to three in the defensive zone, two in the middle zone, and one in the attacking zone.

Objectives: the players take over the positions of teammates and anticipate the action. Improve insight into the free spaces and insight into the game.

Variations: reduce the number of actions per zone (speed of the game, direct play, counter attack). Increase the number of actions per zone (possession).

PLAYING LONG - CENTRAL ZONE IS FORBIDDEN

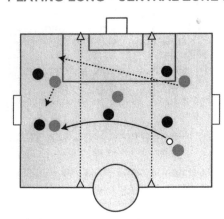

• Half field, 3 zones, 2 goals on the sides, 4 cones
• 5 against 5 or 6 against 6 with or without goalkeepers
• 4 x 3 minutes - 1 min. 30 sec. recovery (stretching)

The players are free to move about. The number of actions (pass, dribble, duel) is not restricted. The ball may not be played in the middle zone.

Objectives: Improve insight into the free spaces and insight into the game. Play long and accurate.

Variations: reduce the number of actions per zone (speed of the game, direct play, counter attack). Increase the number of actions per zone (possession).

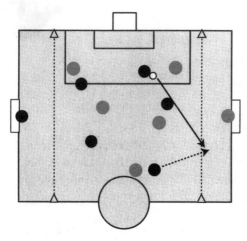

PASS TO A DEEP SPRINTING TEAMMATE

- Half field, 2 goals on the sides, 4 cones
- 6 against 6 or 7 against 7
- 4 x 3 minutes - 1 min. 30 sec. recovery (stretching)

Pass the ball into the opponent's defensive zone in front of an on-rushing attacker. The defenders may not remain in the zone.

Objectives: preparation for the play, ask for the ball.

Variation: limit the number of ball contacts.

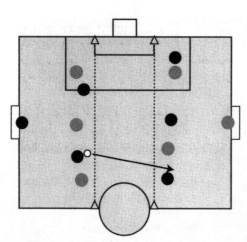

PLAYING LONG - COUNTER ATTACK

- Half field, 2 goals on the sides, 4 cones
- 6 against 6 or 7 against 7
- 4 x 3 minutes - 2 minutes recovery

The ball may not be played in the middle zone.

Objectives: playing long. Importance of finishing.

Variations: the players may not change zones. Add offensive neutral players. Add defensive neutral players.

THE DUELS

Duels make up 30 to 40% of the actions that take place during a soccer match. A duel is either undergone or provoked. It is undergone whenever the player is under pressure (*close to an opponent*) and cannot play the ball. It is provoked whenever a player attempts to go into an opponent's playable space or whenever he attempts to create free space. Through a duel one attempts to keep the ball (*dribble*) with the aim of finding a teammate in free space (*through a pass, a cross, ...*). Through a duel, one also attempts to win the ball back; it is then a part of the defensive action with an eye toward protecting your goal.

The applicable techniques are varied in nature and are sometimes conflicting (*dribble against tackles, ...*). During a duel a player must make a synthesis between thought and action. He must "think" and play at the same time. The technique of a duel must correspond to law 12 of the laws of the game.

In their broad form, duels are played in various situations: over the ground or in the air (*duels in the air*). From this there are degrees of difficulty.

A duel is made up of the challenge of dribbling the ball in a zone that is occupied by an opponent who must be beaten. A dribble requires physical calm, flexibility, a perfect balance; a continuous control over the game situation, over the opponent, over the positions of and the runs made by teammates.

A successful dribble is efficient because the player who performed it has gained an advantage and has beaten an opponent and created a numerical advantage. The player can then play the ball to a teammate in space between two opponents.

1 - COMMENTARY

Teams who are victorious:
- on the average win 53.6% of the duels and lose 43.4 %,
- lose less duels without the ball (22 of 31),
- win more duels with the ball,

* win the duels in the pre-offensive zones,
* lose less duels in the zones in front of the opponent's goal.

Teams who get the worst of it:
* lose more duels than they win (53.6%),
* lose more duels in the pre-offensive and offensive zones.

OPPONENT'S GOAL

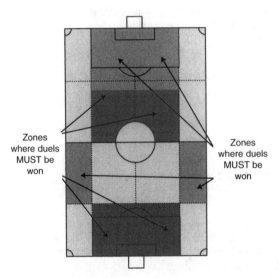

Zones where duels MUST be won

Zones where duels MUST be won

So one must:
* win the duels in front of the goal and successfully dribble in the pre-offensive zone where the attack is started off
* lose less duels than the opponent in the pre-offensive zone
* come out on the positive side in the number of duels won and lost

These criteria are important and are closely related to the outcome of the match.

NOTES: In order to win duels, a player must have all of the soccer technical qualities at his disposal. The duel is the consequence of the foundation laid during the youth soccer development process. It forms the basis from which the player expresses himself during a match. It develops tactical insight as well as the ability to make actions. Winning duels requires developing all of the qualities.

During the youth developmental process, the coaches must consequently place the emphasis on the repetitions and the quality of the duels.
They must not fail to give the youth player the necessary freedom and control the breaches of the rules so that they play within the spirit of the game.

2 - THE TRAINING OF DRIBBLING AND DUELS

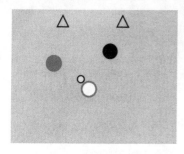

MAKE YOUR MOVE
- Field of 11 yds. x 11 yds., 2 cones to make a goal
- 3 players, 1 ball
- 4 x 2 minutes - 2 minutes recovery

Everyone for themselves.

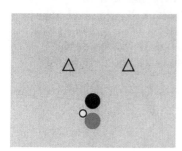

DISPOSE OF THE DEFENDER AND FINISH
- Field of 11 yds. x 11 yds., 2 cones to make a goal
- 1 against 1 to goal
- 4 x 2 minutes - 1 minute recovery
Play may take place on both sides of the goal. Score with a shot.

Objective: create a chance on goal / protect your goal

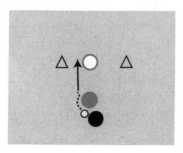

DISPOSE OF THE DEFENDER AND FINISH WITH A GOALKEEPER
- Field of 11 yds. x 11 yds., 2 cones to make a goal
- 1 against 1 to goal + goalkeeper
- 4 x 2 minutes - 2 minutes recovery

The player who scores stands in the goal. Count the number of goals.

Objective: create a chance on goal / protect your goal

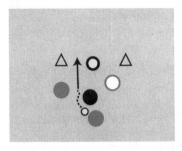

INTENSIVE DUELS
- A big goal of 6 yds., 2 cones
- 5 players
- 4 x 2 minutes - 2 minutes recovery

Everyone for themselves.
Play may take place on both sides of the goal.

Objective: wait for the ideal moment to win back the ball

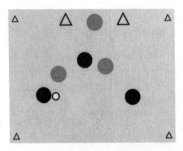

PLAYING TOWARD A GOAL
- Field of 22 yds. x 22 yds., 6 cones, 1 goal of 6 yds.
- 3 against 3 including the keeper
- 4 x 3 minutes - 1 minute recovery

When a team misses the goal three times it becomes the defensive team.

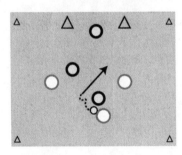

PROGRESSIVE IMPROVEMENT OF THE DEFENDING
- Field of 16 yds. x 11 yds., 6 cones, 1 goal of 6 yds.
- 3 against 2 + goalkeeper
- 4 x 3 minutes - 1 min. 30 sec. recovery (stretching)

Change the defenders and the keeper:
- whenever the defenders win back the ball
- whenever a defender brings the ball under control 2 times in a row
- whenever the defenders pass the ball among themselves three times

Variation: bring the offside rule into play

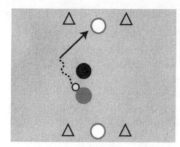

DRIBBLING AND BUILDING-UP
• Field of 33 yds. x 28 yds., 2 goals of 6 yds. with 4 cones
• 4 x 3 minutes - 1 minute recovery
• 1 against 1 with goalkeepers

Players can play along both sides.

Objective: build-up play / disrupt the opponent's play

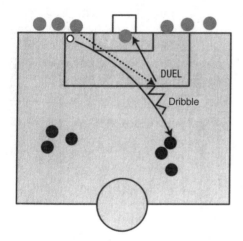

DUEL WITH THE BALL
• Half field
• 5 x 1 minute - 1 min. 30 sec. recovery
• 1 forward and 1 defender

The defender plays a long ball to the forward and then defends the goal.
The forward must beat the defender before shooting at the goal. If the defender wins the ball, he shoots at the goal. A goal scored by the defender counts double.
Count the number of goals scored per team of 3 or 4 players.
The forward becomes the defender.

Variations: the goalkeeper becomes the second defender. Another defender stands in the center circle and leaves at the same time as the defender who begins behind the goal line.

109

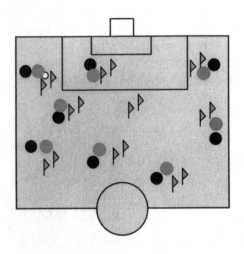

BRINGING THE BALL UNDER PRESSURE: DRIBBLE

- Half field, 18 cones or corner flags
- 8 against 8
- 5 x 1 minute - 1 min. 30 sec. recovery
- 9 gates - goals (one more than the number of playing pairs)

Objective: attempt to dribble through as many goals as possible.

Variation: a goal is scored whenever a pass is given to a teammate through the gates.

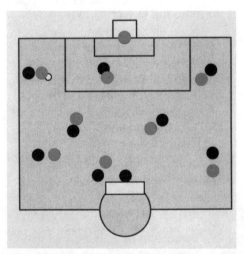

INDIVIDUAL MARKING

- Half field, 2 goals
- 8 against 8 with keepers
- 4 x 1 min. 30 sec., - 1 minute recovery

Every player marks one player and only that player.

Objective: win duels with the ball and lose your defender in order to receive the ball.

Variations: make the playing area smaller in order to increase the number of duels. The defender only intercepts the ball when his attacker has the ball. Introduce neutral players along the sides.

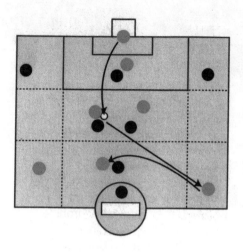

DUELS IN THE AIR

* Half field, 4 cones
* 6 against 6 with keepers
* 5 x 2 minutes - 1 minute recovery

Goal kick from the keeper into the central zone of the field, where a battle in the air is fought.
The player who wins the ball, plays it with the head to one of the flank players who gives a cross to the central striker. Alternate goal kicks from goalkeepers.

Objective: fight duels in the air in all zones.

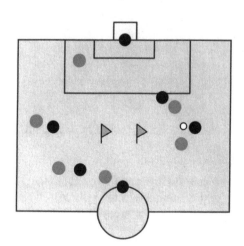

DUEL WITH THE BALL FOLLOWING A PASS

* Quarter field, 2 corner flags
* 5 against 5 without keepers
* 4 x 3 minutes - 2 minutes active recovery (juggling, stretching, ...)

A goal is scored whenever the player with the ball in his feet dribbles between the corner flags.

Objectives: get an attacker open in front of the goal.
Quick ball circulation. Win the dribble in order to gain the advantage.

Variation: The goalkeeper plays the ball back to the team that has just scored.

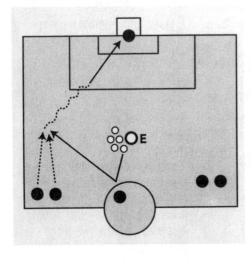

DUELS AFTER A BUILD-UP
◆ Half field
◆ 1 against 1 while running

The coach plays a ball back to a midfielder who brings the ball under control and gives a long pass to a player who is hindered by a defender.
The defender starts when the attacker asks for the ball.

Objective: synchronized movement of asking for the ball after the build-up while being hindered by a defender.

Variation: the defender departs at the same time as the attacker.

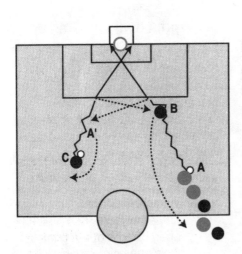

ALTERNATING: DUELS WITH THE BALL - DUELS WITHOUT THE BALL
◆ Half field
◆ 8 to 10 players
◆ 4 series made up of 2 versions

A dribbles B, shoots on goal and defends C from position A'.
B takes a place in the line.
C dribbles A and shoots on goal and then moves to position B.

Objective: duel with the ball followed by a shot on goal.

Commentary: the ball is intercepted whenever the technical performance is not successful.

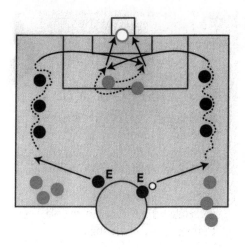

DUEL ALONE AGAINST THREE DEFENDERS
* Half field
* Specific work per post
* 4 to 6 series made up of 2 versions
* 5 teams of 3 players

The outside player must dribble three defenders before delivering a cross.
Every dribble won counts for two points.

After every progression the group of attackers and the goalkeeper switch.

Objective: win duels with the ball while in motion.

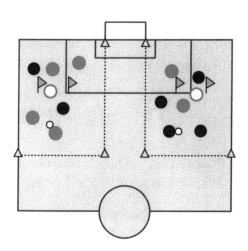

WIN THE DUEL - REMAIN IN POSSESSION OF THE BALL
* Field of 38 yds. x 27 yds., 2 corner flags, 6 cones
* 4 against 2, 1 neutral goalkeeper
* 4 x 3 minutes - 1 minute recovery

The defender who wins the ball back takes over the place of the attacker from whom he won the ball.

Score along both sides of the goal.

Objectives: build-up the play. Disrupt the opponent's play.

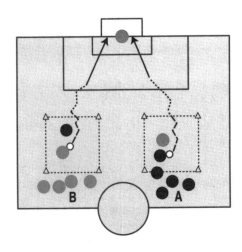

OFFENSIVE DUEL WITH THE BALL
- Half field, 8 cones
- 12 to 14 players with keeper
- 5 x 3 minutes - 1 minute recovery

The attacker from team A, and then the attacker from team B, attempt to beat their defender within the area marked off by the cones.
Whenever the attacker is successful in dribbling over the line of the square, the defender must allow him to freely go to goal and score.
The defenders change after five duels.

Objective: develop tactical insight during the dribble.

Variation: the attacker receives the ball from a teammate. Two attackers against two defenders. A third player plays the ball into the zone.

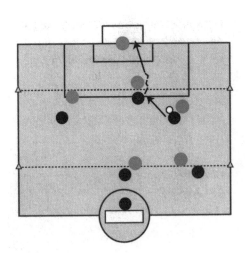

OFFENSIVE DUEL IN FRONT OF THE GOAL
- Half field, 2 goals, 4 cones
- 5 against 5 to 8 against 8
- 5 x 3 minutes - 1 minute recovery

A defender protects the zone in front of the goal. One attacker may enter this zone to battle the defender. The attacker is required to enter into a duel with the defender before shooting on goal.

Objective: win offensive duels.

Variation: the offside rule is in effect.

DUELS WITH THE BALL: THE DRIBBLE
* Field of 66 yds. x 6 yds., 2 goals
* 8 against 8 with keepers
* 4 x 5 minutes - 1 minute recovery

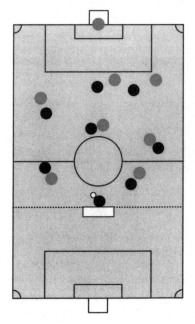

The players are positioned in pairs (*forward - defender*).

Every player is defensively responsible for a player while giving support for a teammate.

The attackers must clearly win their duels with the ball in order to play the ball further or to score.

Objectives:
* Win duels in the decisive zones.
* Bring the opponent out of balance in order to score a goal.

Variations:
* Two players play as sweepers. The others are paired off.
* The coach brings the ball in play in various zones of the field.
* Do not limit the number of ball contacts.

Commentary:
The emphasis for the players is winning the duels (*dribble*). This exercise makes clear the possible advantages of winning duels.

FINISHING THE ATTACK

Finishing translates into a shot on goal or a goal scored. It forms the ultimate expression of the play and is a logical ending of the actions. A shot or goals are the result of all of the other technical elements of play.

The entire team works collectively in order to score a goal and attempt to put the "shooter" in the best position possible.

	LOST MATCHES	DRAWS	WON MATCHES
Average number of goals per match	0.48	0.71	2.29
Average number of shots per match	9.86 (+/-0.5)	10.87 (+/-0.4)	13.84 (+/-0.5)
Efficiency	4.82%	6.58%	16.21%

1 - LINKING UP

The various actions that make up efficient playing sequences are interceptions, passes with and without control, shots, duels, ...

In short, the "model" sequence (linking up of the actions), particularly with regards to top teams, ending with the scoring of a goal, is composed of:

1.7 passes with control + 0.5 passes without control + 0.6 duels + 0.8 dribbles.

A - NUMBER OF PASSES BEFORE THE SHOT

The percentage of shots for top teams in relation to the number of passes:
* 45.6 % of the shots are launched after a pass,
* 73.5 % of the shots are launched after less than three passes.

WHERE DO THE EFFICIENT SEQUENCES BEGIN?

The efficient sequences for the top teams begin in various zones of the field. It breaks down to:
* 22 % begin in the defensive zones,
* 17 % begin in the pre-defensive zones,
* 25 % begin in the pre-offensive zones,
* 38 % begin in the offensive zones.

THE ACTIONS THAT INITIATE EFFICIENT SEQUENCES

The static actions include the so-called restarts:
* throw-ins,
* corner kicks,
* free kicks and penalties.

It is a remarkable conclusion that the efficient sequences that begin with a throw-in result in just about the same number of goals scored as penalty kicks. The same is true for corner kicks and goal kicks.

Therefore importance is devoted to restarts.

On the other hand, the efficiency of every action is different: it is so that 95 % of penalty shots end in goals, but only 5 % to 10 % of the sequences that begin with throw-ins result in a goal.

Dynamic actions are particularly recovery actions.
They include: interceptions, duels, and recovery after a voluntary mistake (offside, kick the ball out of play).

2 - GOALS

TEAMS THAT SCORE GOALS	0 GOALS	1 GOAL	2 GOALS
run the risk of losing	57%	32%	7.6%
run the risk of playing to a draw	43%	38%	23%
run the risk of winning	0%	30%	69%

The number of goals scored by every top club in relation to the percentage of matches played shows that of the losing teams:
* 60 % did not score a goal,
* 7 % scored one goal,
* 3 % scored two goals.

With top teams that won:
* 35 % scored one goal,
* 32 % scored two goals,
* 23 % scored three goals.

A - THE LAST ACTION

The last action before a shot can take any form (*pass, shot, individual action*).

ORIGIN OF THE ACTION	
Short passes - deflections, one touch passes	21 - 25%
Crosses	32.5 - 34.3%
Long or deep passes	10.2 - 14.8%
Shots	1.5 - 3.7%
No passes, individual action	2.4 - 17.4%
Winning the ball back from an opponent	7.4 - 14.7%

B - THE LAST PASS

The "last pass" is the final playing action that takes place before a shot or a goal is scored. They take on various forms; for example crosses, deflections, long passes, shifting the play.

The "last pass" includes 25 to 100 % of the final actions that precede a shot or a goal. They make up the basis of more than 70 % of the goals scored.

The position of the player who gave the last pass changes depending upon the organization.

The player who gave the last pass stands:

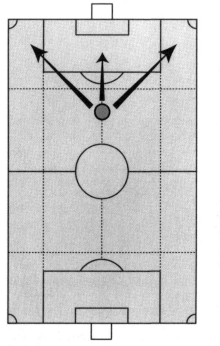 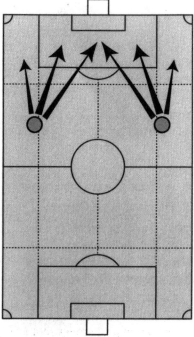

• either in the center behind the forwards

• or as one of two midfielders on the flanks who plays the ball in front of the goal or shifts the play.

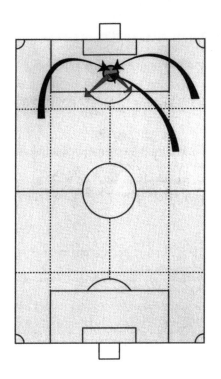

• as a target player in the center in front of the defense who lays off balls for the other striker who is behind him.

C - GOALS OUT OF DEAD BALL SITUATIONS

Dead ball situations are the basis of about 30 % of the goals scored depending on the competitions.

Actions	Percentage of goals scored
Penalties	5.8 - 10.7%
Free kicks	8.1 - 15%
Corner kicks	5.2 - 10.3%
Throw-ins	0 - 2.9%
TOTAL	26.5 - 40.7%

3 - COMMENTARY

The aforementioned efficiency factors of attacking play were measured by:

• the number of attacking and efficient actions. A team takes between 230 and 280 offensive actions, 5 to 25 efficient actions, and scores an average of 1.5 goals per match.
• the efficiency of the offensive actions that lead to goals represent on average .06 % of the total offensive actions of the team. A team takes on average 150 offensive actions to score one goal.

These numbers show the stubbornness and moral qualities that a player must possess in order to score a goal.

The average number of shots is higher after a pass (*quick counter attack, long pass, pass after a dead ball situation*).
A team that wins shoots on goal an average of 14 times per match.
In order to win, a team must enter the field wanting to score at least two goals.
Over the whole season, the best goal differential is an indication of success.

4 - TRAINING:
EXERCISES AND GAME RELATED FORMS

Finishing is performed with the foot and with the head. They form the endpoint of a successful offensive movement. The level of technical and tactical competency, the level of the physical preparedness and the mental preparation of the player influence the efficiency of finishing.

The poorest players increase the power of the shot at the cost of accuracy. This accuracy is depend upon the correct positioning of the plant foot in relation to the ball.

A - EXERCISES IN FRONT OF THE GOAL

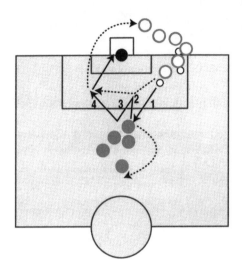

TWO PASSES WITHOUT CONTROL AND A DIAGONAL PASS BEFORE A SHOT

◆ Half field
◆ 2 groups of 4 to 6 players and a goalkeeper
Change the groups after every player has shot the ball 5 times.
1: long pass
2: one touch pass back to the passer
3: one touch pass to the player who receives the ball
4: diagonal pass

Commentary: the emphasis lies on the accuracy of the pass, the synchronized working of the two players and the accuracy of the shot.

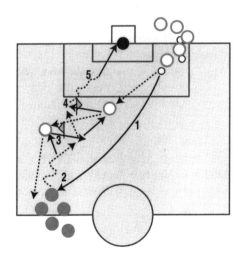

A LONG PASS AND SHOT AFTER A WALL-PASS

◆ Half field, two corner flags
◆ 2 groups of 4 to 6 players and a goalkeeper
Change the groups after every player has shot the ball 5 times.
1: long pass
2: dribble
3: wall-pass left, with the player who has run through the gate
4: wall-pass right, with the player who has given the pass
5: control followed by a shot

Objective: play at the correct moment.
Commentary: the emphasis lies on the accuracy of the pass, the synchronized working of the two players and the accuracy of the shot.

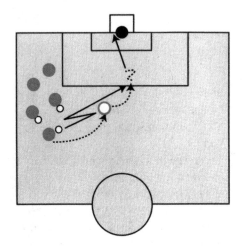

ONE TOUCH PASSING BETWEEN TWO PLAYERS WHERE THE PLAYER IS REQUIRED TO CHECK TO THE BALL BEFORE SHOOTING

• Half field
• Groups of 4 to 6 players and a goalkeeper

Group 1 works to the left of the goal while group 2 works on the right side of the goal.

Commentary: the emphasis lies on the accuracy of the pass, the synchronized working of the two players and the accuracy of the shot.

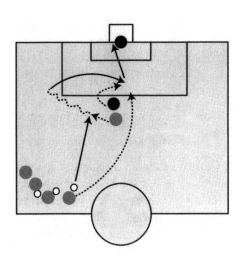

SHOT AFTER A CROSS PASS, A CROSS, AND A DUEL

• Half field
• 4 to 6 attackers, 1 defender, and 1 goalkeeper

Commentary: if the defender does not follow the attacker who received the ball, the coach can place a cone the defender must first run around before entering into the duel.

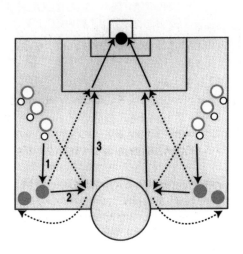

SHOT AFTER CROSS PASSES, WIDE PASSES, DIAGONAL PASSES
* Half field
* 2 groups of 4 to 6 players and a goalkeeper

1: short wide pass
2: diagonal pass, crossing run from the white player
3: deep pass
4: shot

Commentary: the emphasis lies on the accuracy of the pass, the synchronized working of the two players and the accuracy of the shot.

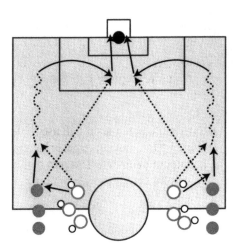

SHOT AFTER A CROSS AND A CROSSING RUN
* Half field
* 2 groups of 4 to 6 players and 1 goalkeeper

Objective: the player in possession is the master of the play.

Commentary: the emphasis lies on the synchronized working of the two players, the crossing runs and the positioning of the player who receives the cross.

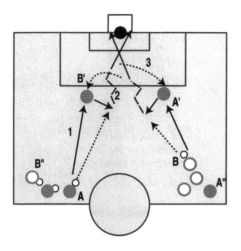

SHOT AFTER ONE TOUCH PASSING FOLLOWED BY CHOOSING A POSITION IN SUPPORT OF A TEAMMATE

• Half field
• 6 to 10 players and a goal-keeper
• alternate between groups
1: *pass - one touch*
2: *dribble - shot*
3: *take up a position as the support player for the other group*

Commentary: the emphasis lies on the receiving of infor-mation for the player who receives the ball, the synchro-nized working of the two players and the concentration of the support players in the play.

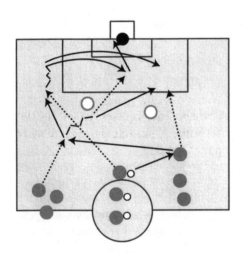

SHOT AFTER CHANGING POSITIONS, DIAGONAL PASSES OR DRIBBLE AND PASSES

• Half field
• 3 groups of 3 against 2 defenders and a goalkeeper

The defenders change when-ever the three groups have performed the exercise.

After diagonal passes, the three attackers must make decisions in relation to the position of the defenders:

• either by-pass the defense and give a cross
• or go through the center (pass between two players, wall-pass,...)

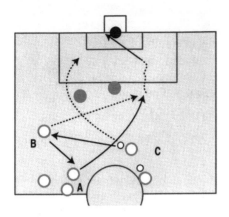

SHOT AFTER CROSSING RUNS AND ANGLED PASSES OR DRIBBLING

◆ Half field
◆ 2 groups of 3 forwards, 2 defenders, 1 goalkeeper

After passes between C, B and A, player A makes a choice between:

◆ **Solution 1:**
After a crossing run from B, A plays B in diagonally.
B dribbles the ball, plays in C who has made a crossing run or chooses to shoot on goal.
C shoots on goal.

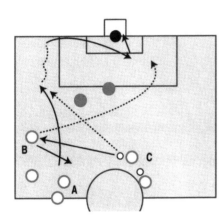

◆ **Solution 2:**
Pass from A to C who has made a crossing run.
B makes a crossing run, C dribbles the ball and gives a cross to B to finish on goal.

◆ **Solution 3:**
A challenges the defenders. B and C make crossing runs in front of the defenders. A plays a ball between the two defenders for B or for C.

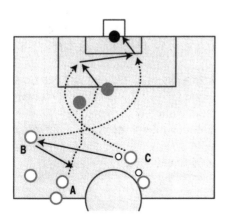

Objectives: make decisions. Who leads the actions?
Variation: the offside rule is in effect.
Commentary: perform the exercise at a low tempo until the players have mastered the different solutions. Afterwards, perform at a normal tempo.

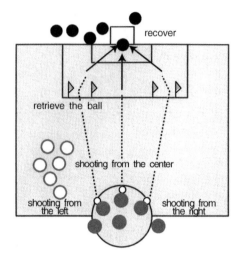

FINISHING AT A FAST PACE
* Half field, four corner flags
* 3 groups of 4 to 6 players

Objective: score a maximum number of goals in a given time span.

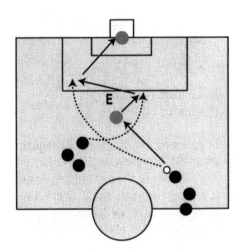

FINISHING AFTER A CROSSING RUN BEHIND THE TEAMMATE
* Half field
* 2 groups of 4 to 6 players

Diagonal pass to the coach. Ball played back by the coach. Crossing runs by 2 players.

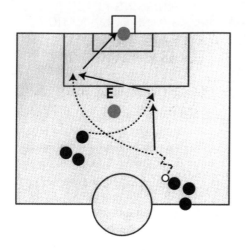

FINISHING AFTER CROSSING RUNS
* Half field
* 2 groups of 4 to 6 players

Dribble - pass
Movement with crossing run in front of the defender

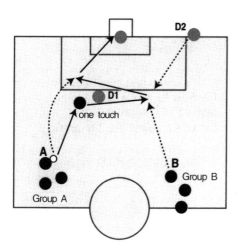

FINISHING AFTER A 3 PASS COMBINATION
* Half field
* 3 groups of players

Forwards: groups A and B
Defenders: D1 and D2

Defender D1 begins against the forward who is standing with his back to the goal. D2 enters the play as soon as A plays the ball into the forward. The forward lays the ball off diagonally for B. This allows A to run behind the defenders.
A shoots and becomes the new forward.

129

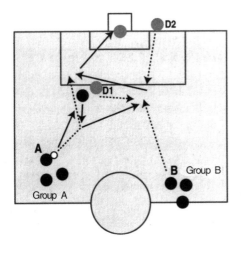

FINISHING AFTER A 3 PASS COMBINATION
- Half field
- 3 groups of players

Forwards: groups A and B
Defenders: D1 and D2

Defender D1 begins against the forward who is standing with his back to the goal. D2 enters the play as soon as A plays the ball in to the forward. The forward lays the ball off diagonally for B. This serves to let A run behind the defenders.
A shoots and becomes the new forward.

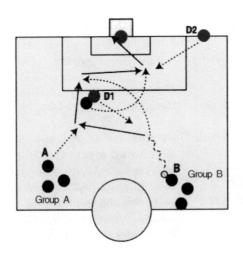

FINISHING AFTER A 3 PASS COMBINATION
- Half field
- 3 groups of players

Forwards: groups A and B
Defenders: D1 and D2

Defender D1 begins against the forward who is standing with his back to the goal. D2 enters the play as soon as B plays to A. A plays one touch diagonally back to B. This allows B to run behind the defenders.
B finishes on goal. A becomes the forward.

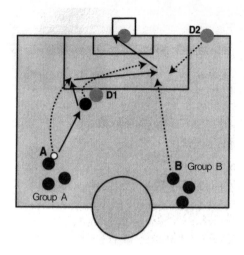

FINISHING AFTER A 3 PASS COMBINATION
* Half field
* 3 groups of players

Forwards: groups A and B
Defenders: D1 and D2

Defender D1 begins against the forward who is standing with his back to the goal. D2 enters the play as soon as A plays the ball into the forward. A plays in the forward who one touches it back to him. A plays in B or the forward who has run behind the defender. A becomes the forward.

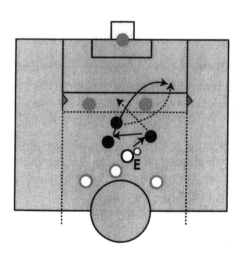

FINISHING AFTER CROSSING RUNS
* Field: the width of the penalty area, 2 corner flags or cones
* 3 or 4 teams of 3 players + 2 defenders, 3 against 2 Change defenders every 3 minutes.

As soon as the two defenders are in position (even with the cones), the three attackers begin with a pass wide and change positions with each other.

The attackers must look out for being offside. If the defenders win the ball, they attempt to play in the next three attackers.

Objectives: getting free from an opponent - crossing runs
Commentary: emphasis lies on the crossing runs.

B - GAME RELATED FORMS WITH A SHOT ON GOAL

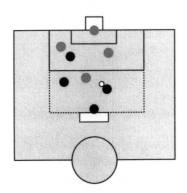

QUICK FINISHING
* Field: twice the size of the penalty area
* 3 against 3 with goalkeepers who play in short
* 4 x 3 minutes - 2 minutes recovery

Free play. Every team attempts to score as many goals as possible.

Objectives: shoot on goal as much as possible. Prevent the opponent from shooting.

Variations: pressure the opponent. Give the ball to the opponent if a goal has not been scored within two minutes.
Commentary: emphasis lies on the quality of the play because these situations often come up in matches.

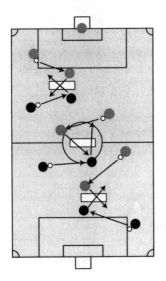

PLAY IN FRONT OF THE GOAL
* 3 or 4 goals spread over the field
* 4 players per goal, two on each side
* 5 x 5 minutes - 1 minute recovery

The player in possession of the ball plays in the player in front of the goal who must attempt to score:
* on the run
* with the head
* with the inside of the foot
* with the instep
* with his back to the goal (*on the run, bicycle kick*)

The ball is then played to the other team so they may attempt to score.

Count the goals scored by each team. The players change positions after five shots.

Objectives: score from every position.

FINISHING

- Full field, 5 goals
- 8 against 8 or 6 against 6
- 4 x 8 minutes - 1 minute recovery

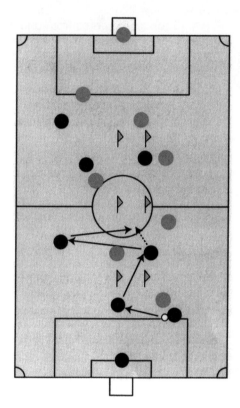

The teams must score in four of the five goals in accordance without losing possession of the ball.

Every team starts in their own half.

The players score on the run (with the head or with the feet).

Every team must score in the four goals without the opponent winning it back.

Whenever a series is over or whenever the opponent wins the ball back, the team must begin again.

Objectives:

- Score goals from out of every position.
- Do not strive for the ideal position.

Variation:

The goals must be scored by using four different methods.

FINISHING FROM OUT OF ALL POSITIONS
* A reduced field, 2 corner flags, 4 cones
* 5 against 5 + 1 neutral goalkeeper
* 4 x 5 minutes - 2 minutes recovery

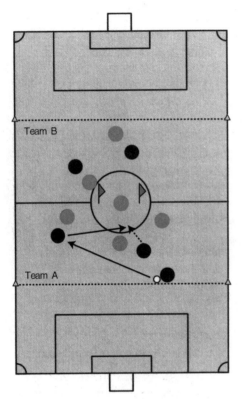

Each team scores from one side of the goal. The players may not enter the center circle.

After one of the teams wins the ball back, at least three players must touch the ball before a goal may be scored. Every free kick will be taken as a penalty from the edge of the circle directly in front of the goal.

The goalkeeper plays the ball back to the team that was defending.

The size of the goal is dependent upon the age of the players.

Objective:
Shoot from every position.

Variation:
Only one player per team may enter the middle circle without the ball.

PLANNING TRAINING SESSIONS

1 - WEEKLY TRAINING SESSION PLANNING

When planning the weekly training sessions take into consideration the total number of sessions per week. For example:

FOR A TEAM THAT TRAINS ONLY ONCE PER WEEK

DUR: 1hr 20min	THEME	
10 min.	Warming up	An individual technical exercise, slow jogging with the ball, passes.
30 min.	Tactics	According to the chosen theme
20 min.	Technique or circuit training	Practicing of technical movements or a circuit of technical/physical training
15 min.	Free play	
5 min.	Cooling down	Slow jogging and stretching exercises

FOR A TEAM THAT TRAINS TWICE PER WEEK

First session of the week

DUR: 1hr 20min	THEME	
10 min.	Warming up	An individual technical exercise, slow jogging with the ball, passes.
30 min.	Tactics	According to the chosen theme
20 min.	Technique	Practicing of technical movements
15 min.	Free play	
5 min.	Cooling down	Slow jogging and stretching exercises

Second training of the week

DUR: 1hr 20min	THEME	
10 min.	Warming up	An individual technical exercise, slow jogging with the ball, passes.
30 min.	Tactics	According to the chosen theme
20 min.	Technique or circuit training	Practicing of technical movements or a circuit of technical/physical training
15 min.	Free play	
5 min.	Cooling down	Slow jogging and stretching exercises

• How can the exercises be adapted to fit the abilities of the players?

• In which order must the exercises be placed?

• What are other possibilities available in order to improve playing technique?

2 - THE DEMANDS OF THE GAME: DEVELOPING THE PLAYERS

The sport of soccer is played against resistances and a performance must be delivered. A child can only meet a few of these demands.

It is impossible to form a team with eight-year-old children, but the coach must have an answer for this. Luckily the child does not have to experience soccer in its entirety.
Thus they may start with smaller games (shoot toward one goal, attack against a defender toward one goal, ...).

By choosing the groups and the exercises, the coach furthers the development of the players.

For older players, the competition is an additional step with regard to training sessions whenever the performances are being compared.

3 - ADAPTING THE EXERCISES TO THE ABILITIES OF THE PLAYERS

Adapting to smaller soccer forms makes it possible to carefully dose the performance demands in the manner that is necessary.

A - CHANGING THE NUMBER OF PLAYERS

A limited number of players improves the mobility of the player, brings him in contact with the ball more often, and makes the playing tactics more assessable.
A greater number of players demands a more pronounced team spirit, a characteristic to play collectively. It should be mentioned that a child understands the abstract only after reaching twelve years of age, which hinders his ability to think collectively before this age.

B - CHANGING THE SIZE OF THE PLAYING AREA AND ALL OTHER MATERIALS

A large field leads to intensive movement of the players.
A smaller field leads to more small-scale actions, asks for self-control whenever someone has the ball, as well as sharper reactions.
A well pumped-up and hard ball demands good control with regards to passing actions and controlling the ball. A softer ball is easier to handle.

C - CHANGING THE RULES OF PLAY

The changing of the playing rules and the emphasis of certain situations only makes sense if the player understands the special demands.
For example, the limiting of the number of ball contacts, which leads to playing collectively and assigning points for certain actions (*shots on goal, ...*).

The least experienced players do not recognize the reason for these new situations. They call upon the coach to make them aware of the objective and therefore learn to better anticipate.

4 - WHAT SEQUENCE IS REQUIRED FOR THE PLACING OF THE TACTICAL EXERCISES?

There are two possibilities to combine the various game related exercises:

◆ You keep to a given theme, for example a shot on goal and defending the goal. You turn to a certain type of exercise: for example shooting from all positions. But a series concept can lead to misunderstandings, because you cannot string together progressive game related forms by only playing. It is recommended that during one and the same training you perform only a few progressions and spread the others over a longer period.

◆ Consequently begin with a simple exercise, for example shoot at goal, then move on to playing attack against defense towards one goal and finally playing attack against defense on two goals. In this case you repeatedly reach additional phases and experience the three situations which are shown in the following examples.

5 - EXAMPLES OF TRAINING WITH PROGRESSION FROM SIMPLE EXERCISES

A - PRACTICAL TRAINING NUMBER 1: IMPROVING THE DEFENSIVE ORGANIZATION

1 - WARMING-UP

Duration: 10 minutes

Exercises dribbling the ball and passing combined with juggling and flexibility exercises.

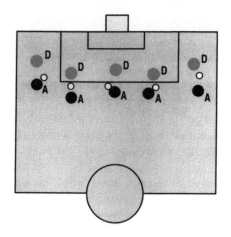

2 - TECHNICAL - TACTICAL

1 against 1
• Half field
• 4 x 2 minutes - 1 minute recovery

The players from team A attempt to dribble past the players from team D.
Players A begin 33 yds. From the goal line and attempt to dribble over the goal line under pressure of team D.
After every go, team A switches with team D.

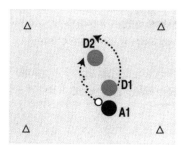

3 - TACTICS

1 against 2
• Field of 11 x 17 yds.
• 3 x 2 minutes - 1 minute recovery

Player D1 attacks player A1 who is in possession of the ball. Player D2 supports him in this. A1 attempts to dribble the ball over the defender's goal line.

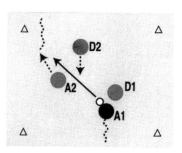

2 against 2
• Field of 17 x 28 yds.
• 2 x 2 minutes - 1 minute recovery

Player A2 helps his teammate A1 against D1 and D2 to bring the ball over the defender's goal line.

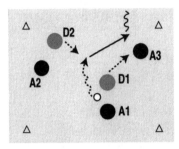

3 against 2
◆ Field of 22 x 33 yds.
◆ 3 x 2 minutes - 1 minute recovery

Three attackers attempt to bring the ball over the goal line against two defenders. If the defenders win back the ball, they attempt to dribble over the attacker's goal line.

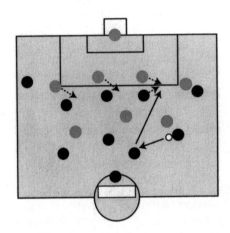

9 against 7 + 2 goalkeepers
◆ Half field, 2 goals
◆ 20 minutes

The attackers have a numerical advantage and look for the opening in the defense.

The defenders apply a particular defensive style (*zone, individual, mixed*).

4 - COOLING DOWN

Jog around the field as a group.

B - PRACTICAL TRAINING NUMBER 2: IMPROVING THE ATTACK-ING PLAY WITHIN THE FRAMEWORK OF AN OFFENSIVE STYLE

1 - WARMING-UP

Duration: 10 minutes
Dribbling at different speeds coupled with passing and stretching exercises.

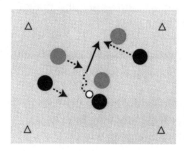

2 - TECHNICAL - TACTICAL

3 against 3
• Field of 11 x 11 yds.
• 3 x 2 minutes - 2 minutes recovery
Limit the number of ball contacts and the size of the field. The emphasis lies on the quality of the pass, winning duels and the positioning of the players.

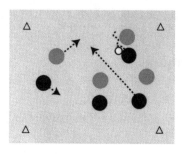

4 against 4
• Field of 17 x 17 yds.
• 3 x 2 minutes - 2 minutes recovery
Limit the number of ball contacts and the size of the field. The emphasis lies on the quality of the pass, winning duels and the positioning of the players.

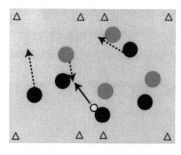

5 against 4
• Field of 28 x 28 yds.
• 4 x 2 minutes - 2 minutes recovery

Limit the number of ball contacts and the size of the field. Change one player from each team at every pause in play. The emphasis lies on the quality of the pass, winning duels and the positioning of the players.

3 - TACTICS

* Three quarters of the field
* 8 against 8 + 2 goalkeepers
* 4 x 7 minutes - 1 minute recovery

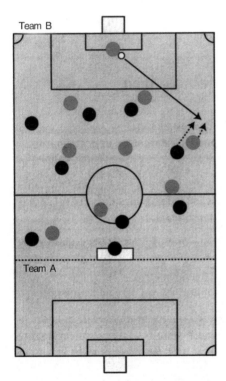

Attacker against defense

The forwards must pressure the defenders and attack the player in possession of the ball.
As soon as the ball is won back, the forwards must quickly move into shooting positions.

Commentary:
Ask for dynamic actions and rhythm from the player.

4 - COOLING DOWN

Stretching exercises and stretching.

6 - A FEW RECOMMENDATIONS TO SURPRISE OPPONENTS

* Make use of backwards crosses
* Teach the players to play in two touches
* Look for 1 against 1 situations where there is a chance of success.
As soon as the duel is entered, one must attempt to win it (it is important to not lose the ball)
* Play together, wall-passes and speed in the movements as well
* Reduce the backwards passes and passes in the width which are not meant to bring the ball forward.

CONCLUDING REMARKS

Just like the technical ability, tactical understanding is a deciding factor. It must be developed starting during childhood so that the tactical insight of young players will be increased and they will understand the learned schemes.

Tactical development is subject to the priority that is given to free game forms whereby the total freedom is given to the young players and allows their creativity to have free rein.

Having tactical insight also means learning to manage all of the risks involved with every situation. One must dare to step outside of the traditional framework without, renouncing (technical, tactical, moral and physical) basic assumptions of soccer.

With this work I hope to have made a positive contribution for the benefit of youth coaches by bringing them a pragmatic approach to the tactical principles and by passing on the exercises that simplify the implementation of tactical training.

This book forms the synthesis of knowledge gained through following top matches and through practical training directed toward perfecting tactics.

P 83
P 95
P 107 <u>U-9 Boys</u>